GUEST OF THE REVOLUTION

GUEST
OF THE
REVOLUTION

KATHRYN KOOB

**THOMAS
NELSON
PUBLISHERS**
Nashville • Camden • New York

Unless otherwise indicated, the Scripture quotations are from the King James Version of the Bible.

Copyright © 1982 by Kathryn Koob

Published in Nashville, Tennessee, by Thomas Nelson, Inc. and distributed in Canada by Lawson Falle, Ltd., Cambridge, Ontario.

Printed in the United States of America.

Library of Congress Cataloging in Publication Data

Koob, Kathryn.
   Guest of the revolution.

   1. Koob, Kathryn.   2. Iran Hostage Crisis, 1979-
1981—Personal narratives.   3. Christian life—1960-
I. Title.
E183.8.I55K664   1982   955'.054   82-18878
ISBN 0-8407-4105-7

*In thankful praise for Edward and Emma
and Herman and Doris who taught Harold and Elsie
about God's infinite love.*

FOREWORD

One of the first times I called home from Germany after our release, on January 20, 1981, my sister Mary Jane said, "Kate, you'll have to write a book. So many people have questions."

My response was a fast and emphatic, "NO WAY!"

I really wasn't prepared for the many offers from various writers and publishers that arrived, and when they did come I simply put them aside. I was not going to write a book. There were too many other things to do.

Thomas Nelson Publishers were very persistent, however, and finally, reluctantly, I found myself agreeing to "just talk" about a book. I still protested that writing a book was much too much work (and it was a lot of work) and that with all of the speaking I was doing I simply didn't have time for one more thing.

After one of those many speaking engagements, I was talking with my friend Gwenn about the questions that had been asked at the end of the presentation. I continued to be amazed that people believed what I had done was in some way extraordinary. I told her I really believed the actions I took during those 444 days were identical to those that anyone who had been raised in the Christian faith used every day to meet any crisis. "Kate," she said, "that is exactly why you must write your story. We need to know that what we are teaching in our churches and to our young people is what will give them strength in their emergencies." I thought about that for a long while. I finally accepted the idea that I had a responsibility to share this knowledge in the written, as well as spoken, word. Here then, Gwenn, is my response to your request for a book.

There is no way this book would have been written without the endless faith and patience of Wendy Ragan and Peter Gillquist of Thomas Nelson. Peter insisted that I could write a book, and then he set out to edit my efforts and turn it into acceptable prose. Lisa Ferris, Bruce Nygren, and Sandy Warden worked patiently with me to produce the final copy. A first time author could not have asked for better or more professional help.

I would be remiss if I didn't thank the numerous friends who read and listened to countless drafts and ideas, but most particularly I would like to say thank you to my friends from Gustavas Adolphus Lutheran Church in New York City who prayed and typed me through the toughest times. I also want to thank Marie Sharps of the *Des Moines Register and Tribune*'s Research Department for her work in locating appropriate news clips to head each chapter.

This is not a definitive account of what happened to the fifty-two Americans. Rather it is my recollection of how I handled the situation during days "on the job" that ranged from a little tougher than normal to downright terrifying. Each of the fifty-two of us was treated differently, and this only tells *my* story—and part of Ann's after we were finally permitted to become roommates on March 12, 1980.

I understand from looking at headlines and articles that were written during the time of our captivity that the going was rough here in the United States. The time inside the compound was tough, too, but often in a way that was much different from the picture the American public carried in its mind's eye.

Here, then, is what I remember as being important in my life from those days when I was an involuntary "guest of the revolution."

KATHRYN KOOB
New York City
June, 1982

U.S. Embassy seized in Iran/
Americans held hostage by students
Des Moines Register
November 5, 1979

1

NOVEMBER 4, 1979

We were in the middle of a staff meeting in my office at the Iran-American Society when the telephone rang. Eva, my Iranian secretary, gave me a questioning look. The receptionist rarely interrupted us with a call during staff meetings. I nodded to Eva, and she quietly answered the phone.

The rest of my staff, all Iranians except our deputy director, Bill Royer, continued the discussion of the film series we were contemplating for February and March, 1980.

This morning's discussion was more serious and direct than normal. The item at hand: the survival of the IAS. The object was to carry out a program that would make enough money to meet our budget; then we could bring back those laid off months before and once again have a full staff of sixty employees.

As I looked around the room, I realized that all these people viewed Bill and me only as contributors, regardless of our titles. The Iran-American Society, or *Ahnjoman*, as it was called in Farsi*, was an Iranian organization chartered under the laws of Iran. These people knew it was to their distinct advantage to make sure the cultural exchange remained alive and well.

---

*The official language of Iran.

11

Eva had proved to be efficient and helpful in my orientation to Iran. Like Helen, Bill's secretary, she was constantly bubbling over with new ideas for programs. Both women were in their twenties, stylishly dressed in Western attire, with beautiful, long, curly dark hair. As customary for unmarried women in Iran, Helen lived under her father's roof, a reminder to me of the ever-intriguing mix of Eastern and Western cultures.

Next to Helen sat Ziba, who served as the manager for the local staff, taking care of setting up various exhibits and lectures. She was older, in her thirties, as was the program manager and the person in charge of films and publicity, Mr. Toorahni. The accountant, who normally would have been at such a meeting, was out of town.

My office seemed to reflect a progressive, yet decidedly nationalistic, atmosphere. I had been in Iran only four months—not long enough to change the decor or add any personal touches, except to arrange several ornate Iranian rugs on the floor for color. The room was large enough to accommodate staff meetings comfortably, with contemporary, brown-and-white striped upholstery covering the chairs and sofas. The large windows near my desk reminded us it was still drizzling and cool outside—the first overtones of a mild winter to come.

It was 11:00 A.M., November 4, 1979.

"Excuse me, Miss Koob," Eva broke in, "I think you'd better take this call." She seemed a bit disconcerted, although I had learned that Iranians are a very sensitive people whose emotions come to the surface quickly.

"Hello," I said, taking the phone. "This is Miss Koob. How are you?"

It was one of our IAS board members, an Iranian.

The ritual greeting of the country was exchanged, but the next words hit me like cold water. "Do you know the embassy is under attack?"

"No," I replied carefully, aware of the staff's discussion still going on. The heavy noise of traffic from the street two stories below gave no indication anything was wrong in the city. "What's happening? Can you give me any details?"

"Not really. But I wanted you to know. Be very careful, please." The caller was gone.

The embassy had been under a series of "attacks" since the revolution: mostly noisy demonstrations, although once in February, military irregulars had actually occupied the compound. But within a few hours, the Iranian government had managed to get them off the grounds. Surely, whatever was happening this morning would be over shortly, too.

Quietly, I relayed the news to the staff. Some of them immediately went to their offices to call friends who worked in the area near the embassy to see what they could find out. Two left for the embassy themselves to try to get news.

Bill and I continued to meet with the remainder of the group. I had come to appreciate Bill's soft-spoken competence and commonsense approach to the problems of the IAS during the six weeks since his arrival. We had heard that a demonstration was being prepared to commemorate the death of university students killed by the Shah's troops in a protest march a year earlier. So when a number of students gathered on the nearby University of Tehran campus this morning, Bill had come uptown to my office after wisely closing the Academic Center.

Sudden closings, irregular schedules, and cancellations had become a regular part of daily Iranian life since before the departure of Shah Mohamed Reza Pahlevi the previous January—they were one of the weapons of the revolution— but life had seemed more normal the past six weeks. We believed today's demonstration would blow over soon. In that light, we felt it was important to continue planning the program for the coming year. We picked up the discussion where it had been interrupted, talking about a film schedule featuring John Wayne and a science-fiction series, and the possibility of tackling something as ambitious as extension credit courses for people who were interested in taking business management or accounting.

13

When the staff meeting broke up, I took the opportunity to ask Bill how the English program was shaping up. Lunch was on the run. I had Eva send out for one of those tasty pizzas from a restaurant across the street—tiny rounds of delicate light crust with lots of cheese and good things on top.

Morning wore on into afternoon, and I became increasingly uneasy. I hadn't yet called the embassy; always in security briefings the polite instructions were, "If there's trouble at the embassy, stay away. Don't call us; we'll call you." We had had special briefings to review security measures after the Shah had been admitted to the United States in October, and we felt we were prepared for this demonstration today.

It seemed strange to be waiting for word from the embassy when everything appeared to be calm on the IAS campus. Maintenance men were still cleaning the kitchen of the center's restaurant, which had been closed since the month-long period of *Ramazan*. (In most Islamic countries, this is called *Ramadan*.) The library downstairs was open, and students were passing in and out, using the books as usual. The student counselor was busy showing a video-tape to a hopeful student immigrant; and Helen was in her office, making sure things were all set for that day's English language classes. I couldn't quite believe there was trouble only two miles away at the American Embassy.

I sat back at my desk, still eyeing the telephone, and allowed myself the brief luxury of surveying the past few months. They had been hectic—and fascinating.

When I arrived in July, 1979, there was an evening curfew, more or less self-imposed but adhered to by both Iranians and members of the diplomatic community. We were home to stay by 6:30 in the evening. Members of the revolutionary guard patrolled the streets, and they challenged and questioned any would-be travelers, especially foreigners. If they found something they didn't like, the unlucky victim was handed over to the local *Khomite*—a vig-

14

ilante group established to rule a local area. It just made sense to avoid confrontation with these groups.

Initially, I lived in a house with one of my colleagues, partly because the other American residences had been abandoned for so long that they needed a lot of work to make them livable again. When the Shah lost power, the U.S. government greatly reduced the number of American personnel in Tehran from literally hundreds to only about sixty-five by the time I arrived. Also, because the political situation was still unsettled, the State Department believed staff members were safer living in close proximity rather than being spread out.

But I was allowed to move into my own house at the end of September after Ramazan, which is kept by observing a total fast from food and drink during daylight hours for an entire month. We kept a low profile at the IAS during this observance, with no activities at the center except English classes during the day. The staff was allowed time off for prayers, and we instituted early closings for their benefit, because the days seemed hotter and longer without food and water.

Following tradition, family and friends began to gather in the cool of the evening, after sundown, to eat the meal that broke the fast. And with the various comings and goings, by the end of the month the curfew had almost vanished. We Americans still did not stay out very late, but gradually the whole city began to relax. One of my staff members hosted a party, which I attended, and there were a few parties and get-togethers at other embassies as well.

By the end of October we were moving toward a much more normal social life in the international community. The American Embassy was a center of social activities in Tehran because of the size of the compound. Covering approximately twenty-seven acres, it was protected from the street by eight- to twelve-feet walls. Most embassy parties were held at the ambassador's residence because it was located toward the center of the compound. That way the noise was

15

less likely to carry to the street and offend our Islamic neighbors.

The Iran-American Society, which was located two miles outside the embassy compound, had been established sometime in the 1930s, when a group of Iranian scholars had invited their American counterparts to share their thinking in such fields as Persian influence in literature, music, and art in the United States.

By 1979, the Iran-American Society had grown to a very large installation with sixty employees—all Iranian—and a campus of several buildings. The Academic Center had purposely been located near Tehran University, so that university students would have easy accessibility to IAS English language classes. The Cultural Center had been built on land that, at the time it was donated, was on the north edge of town. Now it was in the heart of the city. This center included a classroom building, an auditorium, another building that housed a couple of very large galleries, and the building that housed the executive offices of the society. My office as the executive director was on the top floor of this last building.

The buildings of the Cultural Center surrounded a large, open patio area in contemporary design. To the rear of the executive office building lay a large hole in the ground, excavation for our new Academic Center. Plans were to sell the center near the university, for the bulk of our students now were secondary students and adults taking English.

All in all it was a huge complex, and my job was to see that it was put back into working order after standing idle during the revolution.

The political situation was one of the very reasons I had chosen to go to Iran when the post came open. I felt the revolution was potentially good for Iran, and I was intrigued by the process by which a nation would rebuild itself.

There were all sorts of reasons why this revolution should be a success. It was extremely popular. Approximately 85 percent of the people had supported the Ayatollah

16

Ruhollah Khomeini in his return home from exile in Paris. And support cut across class; the educated elite, the poverty-stricken, the Jewish, Assyrian, Armenian, and Christian communities, all welcomed the change. People were tired of the oppressive measures of the Shah, particularly of the SAVAK, his dreaded secret police. The revolution had been virtually bloodless, most of the blood being shed by the Shah's soldiers as they fired into unarmed crowds of demonstrators.

In many developing or Third World countries, a revolutionary leader inherits the problems of his predecessor with no real way to solve them. In Iran, that was not the case. Foreign currency was available—hard currency. Oil had made Iran an extremely wealthy nation, and so there were funds to buy technology, parts, and anything that was needed. There was an enormous cadre of trained personnel, people who were more than eager to return to Iran (many left during the Shah's reign) and contribute to the development of their country by paving new roads, designing buildings, setting up clinics, and offering their services as doctors, lawyers, accountants, engineers, teachers, and university professors. The Ayatollah had said he would be a spiritual adviser. He was not interested, he had said, in the day-to-day political situation.

But now there was beginning to be some unrest. The moderates were very much concerned that they had lost influence. They could see ultra-conservatives taking over, abandoning concern for the building of roads, schools, and clinics in favor of revenge and dictatorial power, using the religious fervor sweeping the country to their own advantage. To the ultra-conservatives, the revolution had not gone far enough, and certainly an element of them felt that, above all, Americans must go.

But private citizens did not always conform to the ruling powers. One of the ironic twists in this idyllic Islamic revolt was the availability of guns to untrained personnel all over the city of Tehran. The atmosphere was almost unimaginable

17

to Americans. During the revolution, the armories at various military installations literally had been emptied by private citizens carrying off "souvenirs." In most instances the trophy was a G-3, the NATO equivalent of an M-16. When the Shah left and the Ayatollah returned, Khomeini announced it would be a simple matter to collect those weapons. He was in for a real surprise, however, for in this instance there was not the cooperation he had expected. People quietly, but firmly, refused to turn in their weapons. I knew people on my staff had guns, and they had no intention of turning them in. There had been an increase in the number of burglaries and break-ins since the revolution, and they were keeping the guns "for our own safety."

The idea of an attack on the American Embassy was horrifying, but despite the availability of sophisticated weapons I was quite sure the students would not use guns. Student demonstrations were normally full of hate and fierce rhetoric, but not a blatant show of guns. Still, two hours had passed, and I had not received any instructions from the embassy. I decided to call and see if there was anything I could do. It was 1:15 P.M. when I dialed the number for the embassy switchboard. My embassy extension had been out of order for about ten days and still was not working.

"American Embassy," said an Iranian voice. That was not unusual; we employed Iranians as switchboard operators. I asked for an extension in the public affairs office.

"Embassy occupied," came the response. Click.

I hung up with a sinking feeling. I knew we were in real trouble. If the demonstrators controlled the switchboard, they were *inside* the chancellery itself.

I remembered there was a direct line to Bruce Laingen's office. As chargé d'affaires, he was the top-ranking official. The new Iranian government had vetoed the latest proposal for a U.S. ambassador seven months earlier. I dialed the number with shaking fingers and was terribly relieved to hear Liz Montaigne, Bruce's secretary, answer the phone.

18

"Liz," I said, "I hear you've got company."

"You'd be surprised what's going on around here," she replied in a voice that sounded strained but, curiously, relieved.

"Is that Kate?" I heard Ann Swift, deputy chief of the embassy's political section, ask in the background. Soon she picked up an extension, and both Liz and Ann were talking. "Kate, Bruce and Vic* are at the Foreign Ministry . . ."

The phone went dead.

My mind was racing. My feet responded in kind, carrying me downstairs to an office off the main reading room of the library where there was a working embassy extension. Maybe the intruders, whoever they were, hadn't yet gotten to the communications area of the chancellery building in the embassy. I knew well that the heavy steel security door could turn that wing of the building into a vault. Liga, the cultural affairs secretary, and another staff member were working in the library office. They waited breathlessly as I put through the call.

Charles Jones, one of our communications specialists, answered.

"This is Kate Koob at the IAS. Are you OK? Can I do anything?" I asked.

"Yes," he replied swiftly. "Call the State Department in Washington and tell them that as of 1:30 this afternoon no one has been injured or harmed."

"I don't know the number!" I was trying to stay cool, keep my voice low, and not cause alarm in the library. There were several researchers working quietly at the tables in the reading room.

He gave me the general number for the department, and I called, requesting the operations center. The response was instant. I was asked to hang on while they transferred the call to the Iran Working Group (IWG), a task force set up to

---

*Victor Tomseth was chief of the political section at the American Embassy.

monitor the crisis. A similar group had been established during the events leading up to and during the revolution. I had worked with them occasionally while I was in Washington studying Farsi prior to coming to Iran. I knew how important any kernel of information would be.

I finally made contact, and my mind shifted into emergency gear. This was no time to allow myself the luxury of feeling emotion. My staff had lived through a revolution and had seen the embassy under attack before, but I knew they could become excited very easily. I had to keep calm.

We set up our operation in the book processing office, also off the main reading room, where we had four phones. A thirty-hour telephone marathon had begun.

I was on one line talking to Washington; Bill Royer, who mercifully had reappeared at some point, was on another talking to the men who were still in the communications vault. Ten Americans were in there. The Department of State no longer could reach the embassy directly, so questions were passed through me to Bill and to the people in the vault. In turn, the response was given to Bill, who could relay it to me, and I would repeat it to Washington.

The Iranian Ministry of Foreign Affairs, we learned, was saying we should just give the students time to cool off. They would ask the Ayatollah to ask them to leave.

"I think it's a sit-in that got out of hand," said Jones at one point. "They said they were just going to sit in, but it sounds as if they've gone wild." Meanwhile, the Americans in the vault were systematically shredding and burning classified documents, the chants of the mob penetrating even the heavy steel door.

Our relay system did not last long. The students began threatening to kill some of the Americans they had captured at the embassy if the men in the vault didn't give themselves up. Finally and with grave disappointment we gave the devastating report that the men had filed out of the vault. The embassy was now completely under the control of the Iranians.

There was no time to speculate about what would happen next. The IWG in Washington asked us to stay on the line and keep feeding them as much information as we could, even though we had lost contact with the embassy. We tuned in the local radio stations, brought a television set into the room, and Eva and Liga began translating reports and feeding Bill and me information as fast as they could. Telephone calls began coming in from a variety of people who were concerned about what was happening.

I took time out to ask the IWG to contact my sister in Washington, to assure her I was OK. If the news was out, my parents especially would be concerned. I was nonplussed when they reported no one answered. Then I realized I had given Mary Jane's office number; today was Sunday, a regular working day in Islamic Iran.

By this time a number of staff members had been in and out of the office—the librarian, the student advisor, Ziba, manager of the local IAS staff, and many others. Some had friends who were employed at the embassy; some had even been imprisoned during the time of the revolution, yet they swallowed their fears and stayed to help us find out what was going on.

At one point I dashed back upstairs to my office for my tea cup, of all things, and met Pari, the director of the Fulbright Commission, head-on in the hallway. Her face was absolutely white with fear as she pleaded, "We thought this was over. We thought we had survived the revolution!"

Once again it was my business to be the strong one. I simply put my arms around her, hugged her, and said, "Come on, Pari. We'll survive this one, too. We've just got to keep working." I never wasted time thinking about horrible things that might never happen. In the deep recesses of my mind I was aware that trials could be held; they possibly would pick out two or three people at the embassy and make a mockery of a trial and an execution. But I didn't dwell on that. I had work to do, and I had to make sure our work was going on.

Throughout the afternoon, we monitored all the broadcasts and phone calls we could. Despite our efforts, we could not discover who the take-over group was. No one was claiming responsibility, and no one seemed to have any clues. Even staff members who had mingled with the crowds in front of the embassy were frustrated in their attempts at identification. (In addition to the student demonstrators inside the embassy, there was a growing crowd of chanting onlookers, mostly men, in the streets.) The invaders seemed to be typically Iranian, men in Western attire and women in the traditional *chadors,** from various Tehran locales and also from other Iranian cities.

Rumors flew thick and fast. The Ayatollah's son, we were informed, was directing the movement of people at the embassy. Thirty busloads of students had been imported from Qum, a holy city some distance away, to lead the march.

My staff continued calling various embassy extensions. I tried the ambassador's residence. "May I speak to the cook about cakes for a party tomorrow night?" I asked briskly in English.

"I'm sorry, he can't speak."

Another try, the direct approach. "Let me speak to one of the Americans so we'll know they are unharmed."

"Sorry, *Hahnum,*** that isn't possible. They are fine. They are talking, reading, smoking. We do not intend to harm them."

One of the staff quickly placed another call. "This is the Texas-Iranian Friendship Society. Please let us speak to one of the Americans." No response.

Our next caller said, "This is a Voice of America correspondent. Could you please tell us about your group? Could we speak to one of the Americans?"

---

*A long, ankle-length veil used as a covering by Iranian women; it denotes modesty.
**A term used like "Mrs."

"We are students following in the path of the Imam,"* said the voice on the other end of the line. "No, I'm sorry. It is not possible for you to speak to any of the Americans."

Dear God, help us, I muttered in the first of many thought-prayers that flashed through my mind. My imagination was racing. There seemed so much to do. And the telephones—would they ever stop ringing?

I held the receiver away for a moment and massaged my left shoulder, which had a sound crick in it from cradling the telephone. There was Eva, pencil slim, absolutely impeccably dressed in her designer jeans, sitting on the floor in front of the television with her steno pad, trading note-taking duties with Liga. Both young women were absolutely intent on doing everything they could to catch and relay as much information back to Washington as possible.

Each member of the staff was dealing with his or her own internal feelings, too. The action at the embassy was being hailed by Iranian radio as a great step forward in the revolution. Many of my staff had worked for Americans for years, and their loyalty was being severely tested. Their faces began to freeze in lines of worry and fear.

Suddenly, about 5:00 P.M., there was a welcome face in our midst. It carried a look of fierce determination. Mehran, John Graves's secretary, had been released. John, the public affairs counselor of the embassy and the director of USICA** in Iran, was Bill Royer's boss and mine. Barry Rosen, the press attaché, also worked for him. The four of us, the only USICA employees in Tehran, had become very close during the short time we had worked together, and here was Mehran to tell us what had happened. We converged on her like hungry locusts. What? Who? How? How did she get away? When did it happen?

She was furious that the mob had invaded the embassy

---

*A term denoting respect and used interchangeably with "Ayatollah."
**United States International Communication Agency.

and was genuinely concerned for the well-being of John Graves and Barry Rosen. Still spitting fire, she described how the students had come over the walls and through the gates with such speed that there was no time to do anything but watch. Swarms of students had moved into the various buildings, tying up the Americans and moving all employees to secured spots. The USICA people had been moved into the commercial library.*

She had been interrogated along with other staff members and finally had been permitted to leave in the late afternoon. Many people had left their cars behind on the compound. Yet despite her face-to-face encounters, Mehran couldn't tell us who these "students" were, either. With a final toss of her head, she settled down to work with us, and we began to send her information to Washington.

Gradually all hope for an early resolution of the crisis disappeared. At 7:30 P.M. a television broadcast announced that the Assembly of Experts, meeting in special session to write the constitution of the new republic, had hailed the students as "heroes of the revolution." This, coupled with the reportedly hundreds of telegrams pouring into the Iranian capital pledging support of the students—some of which were read over the air—certainly didn't bode well for us.

We listened in vain for just one moderating word about the situation, just one small voice condemning the actions of the students or urging caution. We heard only the exultant, sounds of euphoric triumph couched in the rythmic cadences of Farsi rhetoric.

But a ring of the telephone would change our mood. Several Americans who had been at the embassy had not been captured. Lee Schatz, who was our agricultural attaché and had been off the compound at the time of the take-over, had found refuge at the Swedish Embassy. From his hideout he could see what was going on in the motor pool area of the

---

*A collection of books and journals pertaining to trade and commerce.

embassy compound, and we had relayed his blow-by-blow accounts to Washington. In that way we had covered the arrival of the revolutionary guards, a group of mostly self-appointed young Iranian irregulars who had come to prominence since the revolution. They were almost always outfitted in drab green fatigues and combat boots and usually carried weapons. They had lined the gates outside the embassy and were facing the growing crowd and monitoring the proceedings.

We also had been talking with Lillian Johnson, a secretary who had been at the embassy on a temporary assignment. She had worked for the security people in the administrative section, and she had left for the airport that morning to catch the early flight back to Frankfurt, West Germany, her regular post. She had been turned back at the airport because her visa was "not correct." In desperation, she was taking refuge in one of the American-operated apartments on the other side of the compound.

Now word came that five additional Americans had escaped. Kathy and Joe Stafford, Mark and Cora Lijek, and Bob Anders all worked in the consulate. Remarkably, they had simply walked away from the consulate and were now hiding in one of their own apartments. We spoke briefly with them several times during the late afternoon and early evening.

We closed the IAS library at the regular hour, six o'clock, and our English classes at the Cultural Center finished right on schedule. Liga had bread and cheese in the office and made a fresh pot of tea to serve with our meager dinner. The staff left reluctantly, but I didn't want them to stay and attract undue attention to our facility. I asked one secretary, the switchboard operator, and one driver to stay on duty and supplement our night staff.

The Lijeks and Staffords arrived to take over the phones at midnight. We greeted each other soberly. Bill and I briefed Cora, Kathy, Mark and Joe, and then we tried to get some sleep. I took off my glasses, stretched out on a couch in the

25

library, and gave a fleeting thought to my house. It was still new to me, but it was clean and comfortable, and a handsome little place for quiet entertaining. I thought of my big, lovely, comfortable bed. *Oh, how good a soak in the tub would feel!* I wondered what Sam, my cook, had fixed for dinner, although I had called and told him I probably wouldn't be home that night. I sighed once, and with a last prayer for the day, rolled over and tried to sleep.

We won't oust Shah,
U.S. tells students
Des Moines Register
November 9, 1979

2

NOVEMBER 5, 1979

The library couch made for fitful sleeping at best, and all too soon it was 5:30 in the morning, time to go back on duty.

Duty didn't bring any relief either. Those going home had nothing positive to add to what we already knew. No voice of moderation had risen during the night. It was as if the nation had gone crazy, almost as if they were reliving the Shah's departure.

When the Lijeks and the Staffords left at 6:00 A.M., they were still unsure where they could stay in safety. I wanted the IAS to operate on a "business as usual" basis, and therefore I didn't think it wise for them to stay at the center. When my staff, all of whom I trusted, raised questions about the "guests," I explained that I was concerned about what had happened at the embassy, and that these people would not stay with us during the day although they would probably return to help with the telephones in the evening.

Bill and I spent the morning on the telephone with Washington, relaying news summaries taken from the Iranian media. There was a lot of dead air space at times, but Washington felt it was important for the line to stay open. Though there were other Washington-Tehran telephone contacts, there was difficulty keeping the international line free

27

with Lee Schatz at the Swedish Embassy or with the Iranian Foreign Ministry, where Bruce, Vic, and Mike Howland, an embassy security officer, still were camped, trying to negotiate with Foreign Minister Ibrahim Yazdi.

About 10:00 A.M., we thought our line had been cut. Alarmed, my staff urged me to break communication, but I felt we should keep it going as long as possible. And shortly the disturbance cleared up.

At mid-morning, I called my cook, Sam, and John Graves's housekeeper, Neet, who were both from Thailand. I knew Neet well, as she had helped me settle into my house. I asked Sam to fix lunch and bring it to the IAS, and I requested Neet to stop and pick up a change of clothing and my toothbrush on her way. My green wool dress was quite rumpled from sleeping in it. They arrived with enough lunch for everyone, and the strain of the events was plain to see on their faces. I gave Neet a hug and assured her I was all right.

Bill and I hurriedly ate the beef stroganoff Sam had prepared, talking on the phones at the same time. Somehow, there was never enough time to slip off and change into the fresh clothes Neet had brought.

By now, I was trying to help the IAS senior staff prepare for the possible take-over of the center. The Cultural Center was large and well-known, and I was quite sure it employed some people whose loyalty to the revolution was greater than their loyalty to the center. Islam was back in power, and there had been sufficient unrest among some of our staff for me to be aware that our personnel problems had not all been solved. As discreetly as possible, I had someone gather certain important files regarding our status as an Iranian organization into a small bundle for transfer to the home of a member of the board of directors. I remembered the rugs in my office—they were still on approval—and I asked Ziba, who knew the merchant, to arrange for their return.

Bill and I were talking to Washington again at about 1:30 when an employee burst into the room. "They're here!" he hissed. That could only mean one thing, the "students" had arrived—and without the fanfare of a large demonstration, which I had been counting on as a warning for us to get away.

We instantly abandoned the phones and walked out the back door of the processing room, down a short corridor, and out the exit to the parking lot. Mehran and Liga, the secretaries on duty, were close behind. We couldn't move too quickly because we didn't want to arouse suspicion, but we made it safely into Mehran's car. She started the engine and drove out of the parking lot into the busy street in front of the IAS.

Earlier in the day we had asked Dr. Nun, the director of the Goethe Institute, if we could come there for "safe haven" if necessary. The response had been unhesitatingly affirmative. We then told Washington what our plan was, and they cleared it with German officials in Bonn. We had only to go around the corner, about three blocks, but what a change in atmosphere there was. I felt the tension roll away as I saw the relaxed, friendly faces of Dr. Nun and his deputy, Mr. Gussman. One of their staff members brought us some tea, and we took advantage of a few moments to refresh ourselves.

An hour passed. I told Bill it had been suggested we use his house as a hiding place for Bruce, Vic, and ourselves. We had learned that morning that the Foreign Ministry would no longer guarantee Bruce's safety. Going to another embassy seemed dangerous, as the students were threatening to topple anyone who offered to help the United States. We called Bruce and Vic at the Foreign Ministry and told them what had happened. While we were on the phone, Dr. Nun and Mr. Gussman came in and told us they had walked over to the IAS. The students were gone.

We decided to return and restore the telephone link to Washington. Back in the office, we discovered the staff had had a bit of a morale boost, too. They had survived yet another confrontation. I thanked them for their help, and we all went back to work, assuring Washington we were OK.

Shortly after 4:00 P.M., Bill left the center to go home in

preparation for the possible arrival of Bruce, Vic, and Mike. Almost immediately the switchboard receptionist called. "Miss Koob, one of the ladies from the embassy is here."

It was Lillian Johnson. She had spent a terrifying night, hiding alone in an apartment about a block behind the compound. The noise of the mob had gone on all night, and she had heard what she thought were guns going off. It could have been doors slamming or cars backfiring, she admitted, but alone with her imagination, she had been petrified.

I talked with her for a few more minutes, and then she moved over to the phone Bill had been using and began telling her story to the Iran Working Group back at the State Department.

Then another phone rang, accompanied by the sound of scurrying feet outside the library's processing room door. "They're back!" said the caller.

Lillian and I dropped the phones and moved quickly to the back door. Too late! There were students at the bottom of the steps, quietly but determinedly guarding the exits. We turned to go the other way.*

A long-time employee saw us and said, "Come!" Silently he led us down the back stairs to a basement level storeroom and the garage. At the bottom of the steps, we found one door blocked—and more students in the garage. So we went back to hide in the ladies room at that level. There was a window in the restroom, but it was too high and too small. There was no way to escape.

"Stay quiet and maybe they will think we got away!" I told Lillian. It didn't work. They banged on the door. We barely breathed. They left. We took a deep breath. "Don't move yet," I said.

---

*Continuous contact between Washington and someone in Iran ended at this point; however, Bruce Laingen and Vic Tomseth communicated with the State Department many times throughout the captivity from the Iranian Ministry of Foreign Affairs where they were held captive.

Back they came. More bangings. "We know you are in there!" they yelled.

I flushed the toilet to muffle the sound of my voice. While the water ran, I told Lillian to stay behind. Then I moved outside and was promptly escorted by a male student up to the library.

Once in the library reading room, I was confronted by five or six men dressed either in jeans or fatigues, with shirts and knit caps. *I'll never get accustomed to this unshaven appearance, even if it is in emulation of the Prophet's son-in-law,* I thought.

I managed to get the library circulation desk between me and them. It was obvious we would be going elsewhere.

There were people in the reading room, but the students obviously didn't intend to cause a disturbance. They were talking in quiet, well-controlled voices, a sign of good breeding in private confrontations in Iran. In frustration I thought, *I've got to stall. I've got to give Bill time to get away. No time for emotion.*

In a flash I tried to remember all the things I needed to do to protect the IAS so it wouldn't be trashed. Maybe I could talk my way out of this. I asked if I could take my purse, which I had in my hand.

"Take whatever you want," they said.

So I asked for my cape, my purse, and even the white cosmetic kit that Neet had brought, all of which they gave me. My frustration heightened: They had found Lillian. They brought her into the room, and I told the students that she did not work at the Ahnjoman. They said they would release her. I gave her a rattan bag filled with personal correspondence and a log we had been keeping of the days' events. I never saw it again.

As I sensed they were getting ready to take us away, I tried a bolder tactic. "Why should I go with you?" I asked. "How do I know you are part of the group at the embassy?"

"I'll show you my student I.D." one said, pulling out a plastic card from his pocket.

"That doesn't mean a thing to me," I retorted. "Why should I believe you? You could be anyone taking advantage of the situation." They assured me I could take one of our local employees with me to the embassy.

I had maneuvered close to the phone, and it began to ring. I was still not sure how long I could stall. I laid my open purse—actually a slim attaché case that zipped shut on the top—on the librarian's stool close to where I was standing behind the circulation desk. I started to give directions to the librarian about closing the library. I knew she didn't need them, but it gave me a little more time. I kept hoping that Bill was getting farther and farther away.

The receptionist came in and said, "Miss Koob, you have a phone call."

They let me answer. It was Vic Tomseth, still at the Foreign Ministry. "Kate, I hear you've got trouble," he said.

"Yes, they're here. But I think Bill got out OK," I whispered. "Shall I go with the students, I think my staff would resist, but I'm worried about what they might do to the Ahnjoman."

"I guess you'd better leave," he said. I could hear the pain and concern in his voice.

Reluctantly, I hung up. Bruce and Vic were already being held captive, and now I had been caught. Who would keep monitoring the news and feeding information to Washington?

The student militants were getting more and more restless. I knew I couldn't hold out much longer. While I was talking to Vic, my eyes looked down into my open attaché case. There were the keys to the office safe. By now, Mr. Behboudi, my driver, and another employee, Haykaz, were standing protectively close to me. After all, I was the director—and an unmarried woman.

I "accidentally" knocked my purse off the chair with my cape, and as I had hoped, the keys fell out. Haykaz was on his knees instantly, helping me put my things back in the case. I shoved the safe keys to him. He palmed them and then we stood up.

32

But our ploy had not fooled the students. "He took the keys!" one of them said.

I reached quickly into my purse and pulled out my house keys. At the same time, Haykaz pulled out his own keys to the IAS building. We both shook them, and I said, "No, we each have our own keys." I don't know if they believed us or not, but they dropped the issue.

Finally, I could not stall any longer. Believing that by now I had given Bill enough time to get away, I picked up my cape, my cosmetic kit, and my purse.

Mr. Behboudi was right at my side. "They said one of us could come. I'll go with you," he insisted.

I smiled my thanks wearily and for a fleeting moment was thankful he was such a big man.

There was open despair on the faces of all my staff, who had by now clustered near the door of the library. They were acutely aware that their own future with the IAS was in jeopardy. "Carry on," I said quietly. "This will be over soon, I hope."

Head erect, I followed the students out of the library and across the slate floor of the large front foyer. Past the telephone switchboard and the reception desk, the stairs leading up to my office on the right, to my left, large plate glass windows and a bit of statuary that was on permanent loan by a prominent Iranian artist. On the wall of the center I noticed again the poster of a single red rose that had hung there since the death of Taleghani, one of the revered holy men of the Islamic revolution. Once more I wished that moderate voice had not been stilled so suddenly. I sighed and wished for his wise counsel, trying to brush aside the day of unremitting villification of America, Americans, and things American. He hadn't been our friend, but he had been prudent.

They led me outside and down the steps to the waiting car, Mr. Behboudi right behind me. A small quiet crowd had gathered in the street, just as always happens in Tehran when anything out of the ordinary is going on.

The rear door of the little orange car was pulled open. I

33

noticed there were people inside and wondered where Mr. Behboudi would sit. I took a second look and let out a gasp. It was Helen—and Bill Royer. "How . . . ?" I began as I crawled in beside Bill.

"As we went down the steps to the garage to leave," Bill answered, "they were waiting for us."

The door slammed shut, cutting off Mr. Behboudi's protest. The car jolted into gear, and we lurched off toward the embassy in the hands of the students following in the path of the Imam.

3

NOVEMBER—THE FIRST DAYS

The car wheezed and chugged and wound its way through the streets. As usual in Tehran, traffic was bumper to bumper and moving very slowly.

All sorts of thoughts raced through my mind. Were there more students in the car behind us? I couldn't see. Could we get away? If I yelled "Turkish Fire Drill!" and opened the car door, would Bill understand and take off with me? Where could we run to? I looked at Helen's spike heels—she always dressed very modishly—and decided against it. We were probably safer in the car than on the street, where people might be incited to turn on us.

The two male students in the front seat were muttering in low voices. I tried to catch their conversation and then realized they were speaking in Arabic. So they knew we spoke Farsi. I was still in a state of shock—not so much from fear as from a sense of desperation and regret at having let Bruce and Vic down by being caught. Maybe there was still something I could do to get us out of this.

"Helen," I said carefully in a low voice, "when you get back, check that special number and let them know what happened." Would she understand that I wanted her to call the State Department?

35

She got the message. Then I heard her say between clenched teeth, "I'll get him! I'll get him!" She was sitting in the corner of the little car, her black eyes wide with hate, like a regal cat with its back to the wall. I could tell she was very, very angry and very alert.

"Who?" I asked. "Was someone informing?"

She nodded and her mouth closed.

I was suddenly exhausted. "I'm sorry, Bill," I murmured, "I thought you had gotten away."

He gave me a brotherly hug. "No," he answered in chagrin, "they were waiting for us." Helen had run into Bill on his way out of the Cultural Center and had told him the students were coming. I assumed they would use Helen for safe conduct and then let her go.

The car slowed down and then lurched forward again. We turned a corner sharply and could hear the mobs in the distance. I knew at once that something was different. The sound was not that of the shrill, happy, exultant cry of the revolutionary victor. Nor was it the polite, shouted slogans of people demonstrating loyalty to a cause. This was the terrifying sound of anger, hatred, and mob violence. The crowds were roaring as one man: *Marg bar Car-tare! Marg bar Car-tare! Marg bar Car-tare!* Over and over and over. *"Marg bar Ahm-ri-ka!"* Death to Carter, death to America. The hatred was so real, I could almost touch it. My spine tingled.

We continued on slowly, and as we approached the embassy grounds the crowds surrounded us. They reminded me of the mob around the ambassador's car in the movie *The Ugly American*. I was afraid they might attack the car. The crowds were held back by the revolutionary guards, but they leaned over the restraining ropes, getting as close as they could, their faces distorted with anger, their fists in the air, yelling at the tops of their voices.

The car finally traveled the block and a half and maneuvered close to the gates at the motor pool area of the compound and stopped. The chant changed to "Down with Carter" in English. A young woman in jeans, a smock, and a headscarf opened the car door and motioned us to keep our heads down for protection against the crowds. Crouching down, we ran the ten steps between the revolutionary guards into the compound itself. We were herded quickly to the overgrown grassy plot behind the chancellery and told to sit down.

It was still daylight, and although it had been drizzling off and on all day, the ground was dry and dusty. The atmosphere was almost peaceful here, but we could still hear the mobs in the street, yelling and screaming and carrying on. There was lots of scurrying back and forth on the grounds, young Iranians hustling around the buildings, seemingly without organization or structure. So far, at least, I had not seen any guns. I wondered where the other captives were, and if we would see any of them.

The "sister," as we were told to call her, sat down with us in silence. Helen asked if she could carry my things for me. I still had my purse, cape, and the white plastic bag of toiletries.

"Thanks, but I think I'd better hang on to them." I said. "We'll probably be separated."

As I had thought, a group of "brothers," as they identified themselves, soon walked over and escorted us to one of the small houses on the compound. While entering, I caught a glimpse of some of the men from the embassy sitting in stoic silence in the living room. We were led immediately into the bedroom wing of the house. Helen was ushered into one room, and Bill and I were taken to the end of the short hallway and put into a bedroom. Then Bill was taken to another room to be searched.

One of the sisters arrived to search me, but she was so embarrassed by the whole procedure that she could hardly touch me. She was much smaller than I and looked very young, with a round face and a rather pale complexion. Her light blue headscarf was pulled down so that none of her hair showed, and she was dressed in jeans and a gray-checked smock, loose flowing in the prescribed manner. A very perfunctory search was done with gentle hand pats. After she left she must have described to her superiors what she had done, for she came back, even more embarrassed, to do a second search. This time she was much more thorough, asking me to take off my dress before she began, and she finished up by running her fingers through my hair. It was all obviously very new and painful to her. I pulled on my dress and scarcely had time to look around the room before several brothers brought Bill back.

"Don't esspeak. Don't esspeak," they admonished, almost as to school children, and then proceeded to ask us for our jewelry.

Bill, who had simply been angry before, became stubborn and rather vocal in his protests. A small altercation began to develop. It was almost like a scene out of the sixties in the United States. A group of college kids had suddenly come to power, and while the government was still preparing to ask them to leave, their power was consolidating and they were gaining more and more control.

I remembered a rule from a training course in antiterrorist tactics that said, "Don't antagonize," so I asked permission in Farsi to tell Bill to cooperate. This brought a sharp retort from Bill, but he calmed down and finally gave them his watch. It was put into a plastic bag with "Royer" written on it.

Then the man asked to see my rings. "One of our experts will examine these," said the brother, triumphantly, and he handed them to another student.

"For what?" I asked as the "expert" began twisting and turning at the settings. *Not much ransom money there,* I thought. Then I realized that they were looking for secret devices like those used by James Bond. It was all I could do to hide my amusement. This whole incident could have been funny if it weren't so serious. Finally my rings were returned to me, and the brothers left.

By now the sun had set. Had we only been here an hour? Bill and I were both exhausted from lack of sleep, and since a student had been left with us to insure we didn't "esspeak," there was little left to do except stretch out on the beds and rest.

But the room was hardly conducive to relaxation. A constant stream of male and female students flowed in and out of our room and up and down the short corridor, just to look around. This was a new game, and they were all excited about what was going on.

Another student appeared with a tray of food, and for the first time, I was really afraid. *Was it drugged? What were they planning?* I wanted to be as alert as possible, in case I should have a chance to do or say something, though what, I didn't know. For the first time in my life, I wasn't very hungry. Dinner was a congealed mass of undiluted cream of chicken soup, dished straight from the can into a bowl. It sat there and quivered.

Suddenly Helen cried out in the next room. Bill whirled on our guard furiously. "What are you doing to her? Let her go. You told us she was just to be a safe-conduct escort and that nothing would happen to her. You are a bunch of bullies picking on a woman." Bill was livid. I added my bit in Farsi, saying about the same thing.

"It is not your concern. It is ours. Obviously, she lied," was the reply.

Helen continued to cry and sob, "My father will get you for this!"* Her voice grew louder, and she sounded hysterical. Several other students appeared in the hall because of the commotion, and even as they tried to "sh-sh" us, we kept at them to let Helen go. Bill was so vocal I was afraid they would turn on him, but we kept on nagging the students. It must have finally made an impact, for we heard them lead Helen away, sobbing. We could only hope they were letting her go.

The hubbub died down in the little house, and despite

---

*As an unmarried woman, custom would dictate her father to be her fierce protector.

our anxiety about Helen and the continual presence of the guard, it didn't take long to doze off. The windows were covered with blankets, and the room was dark. I fell into a troubled sleep.

"Hahnum," said a male voice, startling me awake. "You must't do that."

I looked at the man groggily. It was a brother named Hamid. "Do what?" I asked.

"Signal your partner with your eyes."

I still wasn't too wide awake, but I thought I knew what he was getting at. "I beg your pardon? What did you say?"

"Your eyes. You mustn't use them to signal your partner," Hamid said firmly. "That is foolish and dangerous."

"I was sound asleep," I said, equally adamant. "I wasn't signaling with my eyes."

My eyes must have been moving in response to the nightmarish dream I had been having. Hamid had seen this and decided I was signaling Bill. So he couldn't see my "signals," Bill was ordered to spend the rest of the night on the floor.

The next morning it was bread and cheese for breakfast, and then two brothers came in and announced I was to come with them. No time for a word to Bill; I gathered up my few belongings and followed them the few steps down the hall to the bedroom where Helen had been held. I looked in and could see no signs of struggle. I hoped that Helen had been overreacting and using the feminine wiles of tears and hysteria to secure her own safety.*

The house was so tiny one could almost touch all the doors off the hall from one spot. As I was ushered into my new room I caught a glimpse through the open door ahead of me. My American colleagues still sat in a circle, monitored by a student guard. I was not permitted to pause or say hello, but it was a small comfort: Bill on one side and these Americans on the other. I would not see or speak to any Americans again for several days.

---

*I learned after my release that, though thoroughly questioned several times, Helen was released unharmed.

40

The room I was moved into was quite small. There was one window in the wall opposite the doorway, and it was covered with a banket. To the left was a dresser with a mirror, and to the right a single bed with only the box springs remaining. At the far end of the room under the window was a desk with a couple of folding chairs and a chest of drawers standing next to it. There was room to move about five or six steps. I could see pale blue chintz curtains on the wall under the blanket but was told very sharply not to open them and not to look out.

I sat on the bed, wondering what was coming next. The mob was still relentlessly chanting outside the compound gates. Then I heard someone moving toward the commissary, pushing a shopping cart. The squeal and screech of those carts was unmistakable. I ganced quickly toward the door of my room. It was shut. I rushed to the window and peeked out. I recognized one of the cooks, looking for all the world like he was making his routine daily trip to shop for food.

As I settled in and listened to the sounds of the house, I could hear interrogations going on. The day wore on, and I caught glimpses of some of my IAS employees in the corridor, being taken to a room for questioning.

Except for the unabating noise of the unseen crowds that continued to terrify me, the day passed uneventfully. The high, thin call to prayer of the Moslem community reminded me that day had ended and the hour of dusk was upon us. *I should have my quiet vespers and worship my God*, I thought. Later that night, still full of questions and fears, I finally fell asleep.

I really wasn't interested in breakfast the next morning when it appeared, but I resolutely ate some and was not surprised when later in the day three brothers carrying U. S. Marine night sticks came to visit me. One wore a red sweater; they all were dressed in jeans or fatigues and were swinging the night sticks back and forth, bouncing them in the palms of their hands to let me know they were in positions of authority. One of them, whose English was quite good, began asking questions. They seemed particularly ea-

41

ger to learn about my professional relationship with Bruce Laingen and just what my position in Iran was. I answered those questions as completely and as patiently as I could, for my job was very public and open. I told the students that what I did was all on file at the IAS, and that they were free to look at the records there.

It wasn't long before I realized aspects to the situation that were almost humorous. More than once a brother who thought he knew what was going on would interrupt excitedly; then very patiently, the one who spoke the best English, would say, "No, she said clearly. . . ." They were so convinced they had a spy on their hands that they were overeager to jump on any odd detail. *Why, these are kids,* I said to myself, *so very young, doing something they think is terribly important.*

The interrogations continued sporadically throughout the day. "Recite everything you said during the thirty-hour telephone conversation with Washington." "What was your salary?" "Tell us all the jobs you've had since you've worked for the government."

At that question I obediently went through the list, starting with Iran and working backwards, giving them dates. The brother who had asked the question looked at me sharply. "You've made that up. It came too quickly."

"No, I didn't make it up," I replied evenly. "If you go and look in my file at my office, you will find a copy of what I have told you. Just two weeks ago I had to fill out a similar request for my own agency back in Washington. That's why I know all the dates and places so well."

They seemed to be finding it very difficult to accept that I was telling the truth. When I told them what my salary was, they didn't want to believe it. They really didn't know what any of our jobs were or how much money we earned. They expected us to lie to them, and I think they were confounded when we did tell the truth.

They came back in at one point and said, "Write down everything you said in that telephone conversation, and don't lie. We have film clips of you and what you were saying, and we have tape recordings of everything that was done."

"If you have all of that," I replied firmly, "then you don't need me to write it down."

Stubbornly they insisted, "We want your account, and don't leave anything out." Obviously, this was just a ruse to make me think they knew what was going on, when they really wanted me to tell them what I had said to Washington.

I almost began to wish I was in the military, so I could be able to give only name, rank, and serial number. Unfortunately, there is no similar ritual for the foreign service. I knew it was important to tell the truth as directly and as completely as I could, because if I started lying, it would be very difficult to remember what I had said. I tried to lay to rest the biggest fear: that they would ask me something I didn't know. They seemed not to understand how little I was briefed on actual embassy business.

Finally, after lunch about 2:00 P.M., there came a lull in the interrogations and movement back and forth. But the relentless chanting outside and the tension inside me seemed to be building to a crescendo. They had brought me a science fiction book to read, and as I've always been an avid reader, I tried to drown out the noise of the mob by reading. Gradually I relaxed until I finally decided to stretch out on the box springs of the twin bed.

The house seemed a little quieter—the students probably were eating lunch. I curled up with my hands under my chin, facing the wall, and used my cape as a blanket.

Grandma had made the cape for me, many years earlier. How grateful I was for it now—warm and cozy and bringing a touch of home to this bizarre, inescapable picnic. I slipped into a quiet, refreshing sleep.

I was awakened by the pressure of someone sitting on my bed. For a moment I thought I was at home with my sisters. If they didn't want to awaken me abruptly, they would simply sit beside me for a while.

Then I remembered I was in Iran. I thought it was one of *those* sisters, and I opened my eyes reluctantly. *What does she want now?* I turned over, expecting to see one of the girls sitting there with her dark blue headscarf framing her face.

There was no one there.

But I knew I had felt the bed move. What followed happened with the clarity and speed that only our mind knows. Simultaneously two thoughts entered my consciousness. They did not surprise or disconcert me. If ever I had been in need of help, the time was now, and those thoughts spoke directly to my need.

In less time than it took me to register that I was alone, I knew I was not. I was reminded that I had a guardian angel who watched over me and kept me. And moreover, at this moment he was also a messenger angel reminding me of the Comforter, the Holy Spirit, God's presence on earth.

I smiled wryly to myself. How could I have needed to be reminded? I knew these things. A half-remembered Scripture came to mind: ". . . but the Holy Ghost, the Comforter, whom I will send. . . ."* Yet a rapid review of the preceding forty-eight hours showed that I had not been very reliant on God. I'd been so busy doing my thing that except for a few muttered or habitual pleas for help, I'd forgotten to call on Him.

My mind flashed back to the days of confirmation when my pastor had laid his hand on my head and, after praying for strengthening and growth in grace, quoted those words from Matthew that had followed me around the world: "Lo, I am with you alway, even unto the end of the world" (Matt. 28:20).

I had reflected on this promise often during the lonely intervals in my life, and here was one more time when I was being comforted by them—and not just by the words but by the powerful gift of the presence of the Comforter.

---

*It was later that I recognized John 14:26 as this half-remembered verse: "The Comforter, which is the Holy Ghost, whom the Father will send in my name, he shall teach you all things, and bring all things to your remembrance, whatsoever I have said unto you."

Several minutes passed before I moved. I sat there, reflecting on the preciousness of the moment. My renewed awareness of spiritual reality had transpired in a split second. I heard no sound from the adjoining rooms.

I seemed to be caught in timelessness; the gift of God's time to remind me that I was His, that no real harm could befall me. I didn't try to sort things out or analyze. It was enough just to know and to think.

The Comforter: One who could allay my panic, my fears; One who could keep me if I waited on Him. I'm not sure how long I sat there doing nothing. Eventually I moved. I knew my routine would change, to be like nothing I'd ever known. Vespers, alone, as I had observed it last night would not be sufficient. God had shown me He was with me always at all times and that I could rely on Him.

Noises began to creep back into the reality of that afternoon. The front door slammed; the students were back on the job, and I stored away the memory of this moment to pull out and think about later.

I picked up the book I'd been given and in a desultory fashion, not really concentrating, began reading. The minutes passed and with them, my mind still running on two tracks, the afternoon. The daylight seeping into the room around the edges of the faded chintz curtains turned deep gold and disappeared.

The minor key wail of the muezzin* calling the faithful to prayer blared from the loud speakers. It was time for vespers. I remembered the American men in the next room. I could hear their muffled voices through the wall; would they hear me? Maybe the sound of the melody of a hymn would help them. I had caught a glimpse of Lillian and knew she was down the hall. I was quite sure she wouldn't hear me, but I had to try.

---

*The name of the one who issues the call to prayer; similar to a cantor.

One by one the hymns I remembered were sung. Quietly, for about a half hour, I sang, starting with one of my favorites:

> *Oh, Saviour, precious Saviour,*
> *Whom yet unseen we love,*
> *Oh name of might and favor,*
> *All other names above,*
>
> *We worship Thee, we bless Thee,*
> *To Thee alone we sing;*
> *We praise Thee and confess Thee,*
> *Our Holy Lord and King.*

And I paused to pray for my colleagues, the students, our families, all of us caught in this mess. "Dear God, help us." Short, but no muttered plea this. A strong cry. Here was my strength.

4

THANKSGIVING, 1979

The next day passed, and the next, and the next, with more interrogations, more comings and goings. And always, the ever-present chanting of the mob outside the gates. I knew there were guns outside on the compound—occasionally the blast of an M–16 rifle split the air—but I never saw weapons in the house.

I was threatened overtly once. A couple of days after I had written the report of my thirty-hour phone call to Washington, several brothers brought the paper back and said, "Did you write this?"

"Yes."

"Then you must sign it."

This is silly, I thought. "No, it's in my handwriting. Why do I have to sign it? You've got it there. I've told you who I am and what I'm doing."

"You must sign it or else," said a brother, shoving the paper towards me. He drew his finger across his throat, the international sign language for ". . . or else we will slit your throat."

Well, I'm nobody's hero. I signed it.

After that incident I wasn't surprised when one of the brothers arrived that evening and said, "You must be tied tonight."

47

"Why? Where am I going?"

"You must be tied," he repeated firmly. As he was quite burly and terribly excited about what was going on, I didn't argue. I had seen him only once or twice, but I knew he was very belligerent and could be quite hostile. He tore a strip off a bedsheet, and docilely I allowed him to tie my hands.

The following morning when a student came in and untied me, he left the strip of sheet lying on the bed. Not having anything else to do, I very carefully smoothed it out and rolled it up like a bandage, tying a piece of raveling around it so that it would be smooth and straight. If I had to be tied, at least it wouldn't be with something that had been twisted into a rope.

In the evening, the same burly fellow stomped into the room and demanded the piece of cloth to tie my wrists again. Mutely, I handed him the roll of bandage. He looked at that tiny, soft roll of material in his huge, fleshy palm and burst into laughter. Still roaring, he left the room to show the others. He never came back.

One tall, very thin man who came into the room to interrogate me was a decided contrast to most of the brothers I had seen. He had an air of refinement about him, was very neatly dressed in a light blue suit, and spoke excellent English. "Are you from the Foreign Ministry?" I asked hopefully.

He glanced at the brother who had accompanied him as if to ask permission to tell me who he was. "I'm sorry, I can't say," he responded. We spoke for a few more moments and then he made a comment that startled me. "I don't understand why the American government is taking so long to return the Shah. I thought it would all be over before now."

I looked at him carefully but didn't say a word. *Wow,* I thought, *this group surely hasn't done its basic homework if it thinks the U. S. government is going to give in to its demands.* I was shocked at his naiveté, but I didn't want to annoy him or any of the others. Lack of sleep had made them all edgy.

Uncle Sam has always made it very plain (it is stated policy) that he will not give in to any sort of terrorist demands, and I knew that my release was not going to come as the result of a U.S. capitulation to the students. *They* were going to have to give in, and besides it was the responsibility of their government to see that international agreements were honored and that our safety as diplomats was insured.

By the end of five or six days, I knew we were in for a long haul. If the Foreign Ministry couldn't resolve this in a week, I was pretty sure we were in for a six-month stay. I hoped not, but it seemed logical since the students were demanding the return of the Shah. I prayed that God would intervene, that He would protect us and keep us and that He would help the negotiators of this conflict find a solution.

In the midst of the political upheaval, I soon got to know the three or four young women who took turns guarding me in the little house. There were a number of young women involved in the take-over who wanted to make their contribution to the revolution. So women guards were assigned to women prisoners to eliminate the problems the men might have had dealing with us women. The girls were anxious to have contact with the Americans and to do their part, but they also loved to come in and sit and talk about the revolution, their studies, their families, and what they wanted in life.

I listened closely to everything they said, hoping they would give me some clue as to what was going on. But they obviously had been given clear instructions not to talk about the take-over and news from outside. If I asked a question about the number of people outside or if an emissary was coming from the United States, they would give me an apologetic look with the prescribed statement: "I'm sorry. I can't talk about that." When it became obvious I was getting nowhere with direct questioning, I decided the next best thing was to encourage them to talk as much as possible, in the hope of possibly overhearing a bit of information.

One little "muffin," about eighteen, was filled with fervor and intense excitement about the take-over. She loved to come in and practice her English on me; she would talk about anything to do it. One evening, about three or four days into our captivity, she showed up with her eyes burning red from lack of sleep. She had virtually no voice left from shouting. Her dress was stained and torn, and her hands were grimy with dirt. But she could hardly contain herself. She moved from piece of furniture to piece of furniture as she talked, now sitting on the floor, her knees pulled up under her chin; now sitting up on her knees to make a particular point of argument. She was just like quicksilver, her hands all aflutter, starry-eyed, and she was grubby, absolutely grubby. Unable to abandon my homegrown role as big sister, I argued with her that she should slow down, get some sleep, and take a bath.

I'll never forget the enthusiasm and her absolute dedication to the cause. "We are going to stay here for a week, or two or three months, or however long it takes to bring the Shah home," she said triumphantly. "I'm not going to wash until it happens! There is too much to do," she called back to me as she disappeared through the door, her dirty brown smock billowing around her.

She was a total contrast to the prim and proper young miss who glided into the room the next morning, wrapped in her long black veil. With a quiet but steely voice, she announced she expected to die on the embassy compound. Innocently, I asked why.

"Obviously, the United States will send its military people in and we shall all die. And I shall be a martyr," she added, her face glowing.

"No, no! The last thing the United States wants is for one of us to die or for one of you die," I argued, thinking of the mob screaming itself into a frenzy outside the compound walls. It would be capable of anything should one of the students be harmed.

These "students" were the visible heroes of the revolution, the demi-gods, the elite of a nation that loves martyrdom. "Dear God", I prayed, "please don't let any of them die!"

The girls drifted in and out. Could they bring me candy? Tea? Shyly one of them offered me a Pepsi Cola. When I didn't eat much breakfast, they were terribly concerned, and I had to convince them I had eaten sufficiently. The sisters ate enormous quantities of bread and rice and sweets, and I decided early on I could not afford to eat all the food they brought, especially since I wasn't exercising. On their diet, I would have become bigger than ever!

The girls talked about why was I here, how I liked Iran. They wanted to know what I'd seen and where I'd been. They found it absolutely incredible that I had never been married. It was a theme they returned to over and over again. "Why not?" they wanted to know. I gave various answers, depending on my mood and to whom I was speaking. My regard for the American attitude of privacy concerning personal matters shot way up!

Their questions about age, the cost of living in America, and marital status were not totally unexpected. During language class, we had been told by our Farsi teachers that such blatant curiosity was customary in Iran and not considered impolite. But I did find all this pajama-party conversation terribly out of keeping with the repeated visits by the brothers. They came back each evening with more questions and verbal threats about what might happen.

Yet, the real threat came not from the individuals in my room but from the mobs of people outside being incited to express vicious hatred for the United States. The students assured me that the guns I heard go off occasionally were being used for our protection and that the crowds wouldn't get in. I was not convinced. The incessant screaming of slogans over and over and over again was very wearing on the nerves and kept me in a constant state of fear.

Several nights later, with the chants of the mob still ringing eerily in my ears, I was blindfolded and taken from my room by several brothers and sisters, with many warnings of "Don't esspeak, don't esspeak." It was about 10:30 P.M. I was told to put on my cape, and I was led outside to a van. Lillian was already inside when I climbed in. She must have guessed it was me. "Hello, Kate," she said.

"Hi! How are you?" I replied.

51

"Don't esspeak!" came the command.

We both fell silent.

The vehicle lurched into motion, and I followed the routing in my head, as I was familiar with the embassy grounds. We came to a sudden stop, and Lillian and I were marched into a building.

Still blindfolded, I was led by a sister to a corner of a room, tossed a blanket, and told to sleep with my blindfold on.

"I'll try, but I can't make sure it won't come off in the night," I said to the direction of the sister. Our captors must have seen what a ridiculous idea this was, for they soon removed the blindfold, with many admonitions not to look around.

The lights were ablaze in the room, and I barely had a chance to see we were in the living room of the ambassador's residence before I pulled the blanket over my head to sleep. American and Iranian women were stretched out all over the floor, as if someone had arranged for a gigantic slumber party. As I closed my eyes I realized that in the rush I had left behind my toothbrush and comb—all I had been given from my toiletries bag.

I had little chance to survey the situation until the following morning when we were awakened about 6:30. When monitoring the take-over from the IAS, we had been given the impression that the hostages were seeing each other. We had been assured by the students that the hostages were free to talk, move around the room, and carry on conversations. But now I saw this was not true at all, not just in my case but for everyone.

The other American women and I were tied with strips of sheets to dining room chairs with straight backs and arms. One eagle-eyed sister sat right beside each of us, watching very sharply to see that we looked straight ahead and not at each other. We were not permitted to talk to each other, and it was only possible through voice identification to try to sort things out. I could tell right off that Ann Swift was to my left, but soon they were afraid that Ann and I were trying to communicate with each other. I was moved to another location in the room, this time facing the wall to the right of the fireplace. Kathy Gross was to the left of the fireplace, and I eventually determined that Liz Montaigne was by the grand piano to my right.

The American women in the room were the ones who were on the compound at the time of the take-over, which was not surprising. There were seven of us in all, and I was just awfully glad to see that we were all in the same room. Even though we couldn't speak to each other, somehow there was strength in knowing that they were all alive, that they had all survived, and that we were together.

How long had the others been in this room? How long would we stay? As this day wore on quietly—breakfast of bread and cheese, a lunch of American food—it was obvious that we would be here for a while. I began to look for scraps of hope. It was frustrating to be so close to the rest of these women and not be able to reach out and comfort them. I knew they were going through all sorts of private agony, and I could hear from their voices that their reactions to stress were all different.

I had a chance to look around the room when I was led to the toilet. All of the beautiful furniture and lamps had been shoved into a pile and the luxuriant carpets on the floor rolled up and moved aside. The sisters had no qualms about walking over them. Furniture had been carelessly broken, and of course there was the ubiquitous writing on the walls that seemed to be the trademark of the Iranian revolution. I couldn't believe the disregard for lovely things our captors had displayed.

I had attended an embassy Halloween party in this same room three days before the take-over, and incongruously, witches and jack-o-lanterns and haunted houses still grinned at us from the walls under the crystal chandeliers, as if to taunt us with memories of our wonderful party with the diplomatic community. Now here we were, sitting bound to

53

these hard chairs, in a bizarre, silent circle on the polished hardwood floor.

The guards brought us books later in the day and tied our hands loosely enough to manipulate the pages. I was all right as long as I had books; they helped me keep my equilibrium.

But how about Joan? Terry? What were they doing if they didn't like to read?

It was all too strange to take in anyway; at first I spent hours just listening to the sounds of the revolution outside the residence—always the chanting. I soon realized, too, the students delighted in dropping words like "execution" and "trial" in our hearing. "Execution" was enough to remind one of the most feared name in Iran—Halkhali, the so-called hanging judge. Just the suggestion that he might be near the embassy compound was enough to send shudders through my body. The man was without mercy.

Our captors loved to smile mysteriously as they moved us about, making an elaborate production of the most routine things. The more mystery they could conjure up, the happier they were.

The day wore on. The drapes were pulled at the windows, and I struggled to keep track of how long I had been sitting. Two hours? Four? I thought of my parents. Mother and Daddy lived alone in their retirement home on our family farm in Iowa. They both had had strokes. How had this affected them? How much did they know? I thought about my sisters—Micki, Vivian, Anabeth, Mary Jane, Emi—scattered across the United States with their husbands and children; Mary Jane in Washington with her work. I knew that the girls would do everything they could, and I was so grateful I had a large family to help each other through this time.

But what *was* happening? Mother and Daddy cared about me very much. Would this be more than their systems could stand? Somehow, having been captured, I was convinced I was contributing to their ill health.

As I grew more tired and restless, I decided to pray for

every captive I knew by name. They had to be as frustrated as I was. I shifted, and shifted again, trying to find just one soft spot in the seat of that hardwood chair.

Finally (it seemed an eternity) we were handed a blanket. One of the sisters stood and announced, "It is now 10:30; you may sleep." In ritual, we were untied from the chairs and motioned to sit on our blanket on the floor. My neck ached, my back was sore, and I had long ago lost the feeling in my legs. My green wool dress was clammy and limp from wear. How long had it been since I bathed? I had been permitted a shower in the little house, but I was too tired now to count how many days ago.

A sister came by and re-tied my wrists loosely, then covered me with another blanket. Sleep didn't come easily, but at least I could pull the blanket over my head, and I didn't have to look at the sisters. I didn't have to look at their chadors or the looks of exultation on their faces, which was so repugnant. They were so excited and so convinced that they had done something marvelous and wonderful; yet we were simply diplomats who were trying in the best way we knew how to reestablish a sound relationship between the new Islamic Republic of Iran and the United States.

The next day came and went, and the next. Books, silence, the rustle of chador behind me. Stare at the wall, straight ahead. Listen to the chants outside.

One of the chants the students shouted over and over and over contained words that sounded, at least to my ears, like a call to Halkhali to come to the embassy and take care of us. The edge of horror sharpened each day.

On the fifth night in this location, I determined to wash out my undies and stockings, putting them back on damp. Surprisingly, they dried quickly next to my warm skin. But I made the mistake of sneezing once or twice, and by morning, the sisters had piled four or five blankets on top of me, concerned that I had a cold. I woke hot and sweaty and uncomfortable. *The only danger here will be death by suffocation,* I decided.

After breakfast of bread and cheese the sister blind-

55

folded me and led me to a bathroom for a shower and a chance to wash my hair. A real treat, despite the filth in the bathroom. So many of us piled up in one building put a tremendous strain on the facilities. This was coupled with the fact that customs in Iran are quite different from ours. One I never could accept was the idea of throwing used toilet paper on the floor (and finally months later into a receptacle) so that it wouldn't "clog the toilet." In addition, the students apparently were not accustomed to cleaning up after themselves. It was not uncommon to find that they had stood on the toilet seat letting their feces and urine splatter at will and then simply had walked off leaving the mess for the next comer, most likely an American to be sure.

Coming back from the toilet, I passed close enough to Liz Montaigne to give her a squeeze on the shoulder as I walked by. I was able to catch glimpses of the other women as they came back from their baths.

The only way I knew how the others were doing was when one of us spoke to one of the guards, and of course, the guards wanted us to speak very quietly so the others couldn't hear. Lillian must have had a cold or a sore throat because she kept asking for water. I knew several of the others were tense, too. Sometimes I heard a sharp voice as someone would ask something; other times I could just feel the tension in the room. One day Kathy was crying; I never learned why.

My comb and toothbrush had been retrieved from the little house, and freshened by the bath, I asked one of the sisters to go to the Ahnjoman and bring me my jogging suit and a T-shirt. I kept them in the office for late afternoon tennis games. They would certainly have been more comfortable than my dress for sitting all day.

"I will see if it is permitted," she said blankly, her dark eyes revealing no emotion. The jogging suit never appeared.

Finally, I asked for at least a needle and thread. My stockings had developed several rather large runs. The sisters brought me whatever color of thread they could find, and I stitched them together as best I could.

A they're-not-going-to-get-us attitude began to set in. We'd survived this long, and though they were threatening trials and executions, each day we survived was to our benefit. I decided the challenge each morning was to get through the day. *Only focus on what is happening today,* I told myself. But as the days came and went, I inevitably spent hours thinking about my family and friends and going over and over the scenario back at the IAS. What had I done wrong? How should I have done things differently? How could I possibly have let Bill and Lillian be captured? How could I have let Vic and Bruce down by being captured? *Now, stop it; this is doing no good.* . . . Could I have gotten out another way? Was there another exit I overlooked? I walked the corridors of the Cultural Center in my mind again and again. Was there something else I should have done?

The few times I could shake these feelings of guilt were when we were permitted to exercise. I began to realize our captors wanted to keep us healthy. One by one we were allowed to go to the center of the room for ten minutes of calisthenics, while the rest of us sat mutely in our chairs around the edge of the room, reading or daydreaming or staring at the wall.

I drew comfort from small victories. *Retain control of as much as you can.* The midday meal was good, often familiar food like hot dogs and potato salad, spaghetti and meat balls, hamburgers and french fries. It all came from the co-op, a store located on the embassy compound that carried American food and other items, and was prepared by the Pakistani cook who had agreed to stay behind. But the evening meals were still being prepared by the students—unheated, tasteless messes of canned ravioli or cream-of-something soup. My repeated offers to help cook were firmly rejected with protests of "No, you are our guest, Hahnum." *But you can control this part of your life. You don't have to eat all that they bring,* I reminded myself. I continued to diet, aiming at keeping up my strength while losing at least five pounds.

Then there was the matter of sleeping tied up. There is

no way to sleep comfortably with one's hands tied. I quickly discovered the knots were easy and soon slept in comparative freedom, always careful to hide my arms under the blankets and secure my hands again first thing in the morning.

Another frustration came with my encounter with "Queenie," as I nicknamed her. After about ten days, a very haughty, stocky woman obviously used to giving orders brought me a change of clothing: a pair of blue polyester slacks, a red knit shirt, and a tan pullover sweater. She did not bring me any underclothes. When I asked for clean ones, she shrugged her shoulders in the inimical Iranian way and answered, "*Miad.*" It is coming.

After a couple of days without undies, I tried again. "Where are my clothes? I would like my underclothing."

"They are being washed."

"Can you find me some in the commissary?"

"*Miad.*"

"You said that two days ago." In desperation I tried a different tactic. "In my country, only whores go without underclothing," I snapped. "I would like some panties and a bra. I am as embarrassed to go around without underclothing as you are to go out in public without your chador."

That worked. Some undies were found—a pair of panties and my own bra. I said thank you and made myself comfortable.

Then, one by one, the other American women began to disappear from the room for lengthy periods. A sister would walk in and say, "Come." Then the blindfold was tied in place, and the American was led from the room. There was no indication where she was taken or how long she would be gone, but I was glad when she returned. Often the woman looked exhausted when she came back, or I heard a sigh of despair. In a few more days, however, one of them was taken and she did not return. The next night, after we had gone to bed, I heard noises and figured out that one by one the other women were being moved. What was happening?

They must be going home, I concluded with delight. The

other women, with the exception of Ann, were all secretaries. I hoped very much they would release all the embassy staff people. I thought about the young Marines who were embassy guards—only in their twenties—and then I thought of Bill Royer again. Where was he?

My turn came around midnight, after we had stretched out to sleep. I was roused with great mystery and shushings, blindfolded with my neck scarf, and moved across the hall; my hands were still tied. I barely had had time to grab my toothbrush and comb. When my blindfold was removed, I could see we were in the residence library, a small, elegant room painted yellow, with pale blue drapes. Most of the books had been removed from the shelves and the beautiful painting of calligraphy that had been above the fireplace was gone. In fact, I realized with a rush, all the pictures in the house had been taken off the walls. A handsome, ornate secretary had been moved in front of the fireplace, and the rest of the furniture had been pushed against the walls. Any semblance to a comfortable reading room had been completely destroyed. Cushions were on the wrong chairs. *Why did they do that?* I asked myself. The piano was across the hall, but senselessly the piano bench had been dragged in here.

There were three French doors, one with bookshelves on either side at the far end of the room, and two on the outside wall. Any idea of escape was quickly negated as I picked up the sound of the guard moving up and down on patrol duty outside those windows. I was given my blanket and told to sleep at one end of the room.

Then, almost on cue, the room began to fill up with sisters. They were soon stretched out side by side, sleeping, chattering, praying, reading, brushing their hair, doing the thousand and one things young women do. One had washed her gloves and was smoothing them out to dry. They continued to come in, grabbing blankets and pillows off the couches or crawling up on a pillowless couch. There must have been twenty or thirty girls all together, literally wall-to-wall bodies.

The commotion finally died down, or I fell asleep. I really didn't know which happened first. But all too soon I heard them waking each other to remind themselves about early morning prayers. One of the brothers knocked at the door, and the girls shrieked and screamed as they leaped for their chadors. They couldn't be seen with their heads and clothes uncovered. A few minutes later, one of the brothers opened the door to ask something, and one girl in jeans and loose flowing shirt with a headscarf on screamed in mock horror. She was standing there without her chador. Conscientiously, the girls continued to wake each other so they could assume posts, gate duty and guard duty and duty answering the telephone. It was one big giggle as far as they were concerned, and I lay there with my face to the wall, listening to it all. I certainly was never offered a couch or a cushion to sleep on! I finally fell asleep again, singing softly to myself:

> *Have thine own way, Lord.*
> *Have thine own way.*
> *Thou art the Potter.*
> *I am the clay.*

The quiet woke me. "Thank You, Lord for keeping me safe. Help me face today."

I realized my hands were no longer tied, but I listened very carefully before moving. The room sounded almost empty. Cautiously I opened my eyes and shifted the blanket so I could see a bit. Most of the sisters had gone. There was someone at the other end of the room. Was it Ann? I stirred a bit.

"Good morning, Hahnum Koob," the sister said.

"Good morning. May I go to the bathroom?" I asked. When the sister nodded, I picked up my toothbrush and she led me blindfolded out of the room, but not before I had confirmed that Ann was with me. The other women were nowhere to be found.

I was brought back to the room and seated in a large,

black armchair facing the wall, a welcome change from that hard dining room chair. Ann was in a similar chair facing the wall at the other end of the room. We were no longer tied up—another marvelous relief—and could keep track of time by the sisters' radios, but we were forbidden to speak to each other.

Queenie was in charge of as much as she could manage. She loved to be in on the decision-making, and I was sure she was terribly frustrated when she was not elected to the student's general council. But she kept trying to do things that would convince people of her importance, and much of that took the form of questioning me.

Several days after we had been moved into the residence library, Ann was escorted to the shower and I was left alone with Queenie.

"What do you report to Miss Swift?" she inquired.

"I don't report to Miss Swift. I report to Mr. Graves, my supervisor," I answered.

"Miss Swift says you report to her. What kinds of things do you tell her about?"

"I don't report to Miss Swift," I repeated.

"She says you do. Are you calling her a liar?"

Dilemma. I was confident Ann had not said I reported to her, but I couldn't be sure of what she had said. Clearly, Queenie was trying to play us off, one against the other.

"I really don't know what she could be talking about," I said carefully, "unless you consider that occasionally I may share some information with her, like the opening dates of the university. But the only person I report to in the embassy is my boss, Mr. Graves."

Ann came back into the room, and our exchange ended. For a time.

On November 22, Thanksgiving morning, Ann and I woke up simultaneously. *I'm supposed to be in India right now for that Fulbright conference*, I thought. *What would Ann be doing if we weren't here?* We looked at each other across the room and offered mute consolation with a smile that said, "Hang in there!"

It's good that we did. That night Ann was moved, with all the abruptness and hush-hush flurry of activity that accompanied such incidents. Without even a chance to say good-bye, I was alone again.

Shah arrives in Panama/
Angry Iranians threaten to
move quickly on spy trials
Des Moines Register
December 16, 1979

5

DECEMBER, 1979

What had happened to Ann? Would she come back? I had just had a glimpse of her before I went to sleep, sitting up in her chair, blindfolded and waiting. How awful. The day after she was led away was terribly long. And the next. And the next. Ann didn't return.

I assumed we were being moved for a variety of purposes. Obviously, all the women had been kept together originally so we would be easy to take care of. Now we probably were being moved so that no one would have a clear picture of where we were, if anybody was giving reports outside. Perhaps in a few more days we would be moved back into the chancellery into some room where we might be asked to identify certain items or make comments about "spy" equipment or correspondence that had been unearthed in the building.

But it soon became clear to me there was no reason behind the moves. They were entirely up to the whim of the kids. The kids—many of them were young enough to be my daughters—had told me I would not be beaten or mistreated, and each day that things continued as before, I believed we were a little better off.

I knew Islam's respect for unmarried women and so had

63

no fear of molestation by the brothers. They would not even touch me when I was being led from room to room: They always called for a sister or towed me on the end of a handkerchief. The biggest fear was not knowing what the future held and not knowing what was happening to my colleagues. And then there was the undercurrent: threats of trials and executions. The stress was intense.

I heard lots of comings and goings while sitting alone in that residence library, facing the wall, though precious little information. I heard the girls rustle out to the council meetings where the manner of life on the compound was being determined. I listened to them return and discuss those meetings and the Arabic lessons they were taking. One night I heard the magic initials CBS, NBC, and ABC. The sisters refused to tell me what went on at those newscasts, but one of them did say with a smile: "All of them are there . . . they're all there. And we're telling them our side of the story." I was elated to know our correspondents were on hand. That meant our people back home, including my family, were learning about what was happening to us.

One day shortly after Ann left, I heard a new set of noises. I couldn't figure out what it was at first. Then I knew. Someone was crawling around in the cold air ducts, looking for "secret equipment." I wondered whether they were going to tear down the whole heating unit as they climbed through the giant pipes. When they banged on the register, it was all I could do to resist the temptation to bang back a furious reply. But I sat there clenching my fists, listening, full of rage. I had caught glimpses of other rooms in the house by peering under my blindfold when being taken back and forth from the toilet. These kids—they were so young!—seemed bent on wanton destruction. They had absolutely demolished the beautiful furnishings of the ambassador's residence, and much had been completely destroyed. Furniture had been taken apart and broken, left outside in the rain, pictures simply disappeared, and cushions had been carelessly strewn about and trod upon with heavy boots. There was barely a wall that had not been written on with Magic

Marker. The slogans reminded me of graffiti in a New York subway.

One incident amused me, though. A sister had taken a black Magic Marker and had written on a pair of handsome wooden cabinet doors in the library "Down with the Carter." (Their English wasn't always perfect.) A few days later another girl, who couldn't see too well, took a beautiful colored portrait of Khomeini—there were posters of their idol everywhere—and stuck it up on the cabinet. She should have been more careful placing it, for when I looked again I saw "Down with" and the picture of the Ayatollah. I was amused by that sight for a long time.

By now autumn was moving into winter, and the sisters were terribly concerned about whether or not I was warm enough. They moved my chair, deciding I should sit at the other end of the room, and brought in an electric heater, which they promptly used as a clothes dryer.

I was nearer the windows, but with the heavy drapes it made little difference. The overhead light was on day and night, but by observing the girls' comings and goings, watching the slip of light that crept across the floor from under the heavily shrouded windows, and listening for the evening call to prayer I kept track of the passage of days.

In a few more days, the sisters were given possession by the brothers of the big reception room in the residence. With many giggles and much excitement, they moved all the usable furniture out of the library, leaving only my armchair in one corner and a straight-backed chair in the middle of the room for whoever was on guard duty. It was lonely at first, after the constant hubbub of the slumber parties, but much less tiring in the long run.

In the relative calm, I realized I had to do something more constructive with my time. I was allowed to stand up and exercise for ten minutes a day. While I never have been an exercise enthusiast (my favorite exercise is turning the page of a book), I knew it was important. So I thought back to my high school gym class and drew on the calisthenics that I had learned there. I also remembered a set of six-

65

minute exercises that I had found several years before in *McCall's*. They had stood me in good stead before a vigorous skiing holiday.

Then I tried to recall everything I had read about isometrics. I exercised in my chair, flexing and relaxing muscles. I thought about acting classes that focused on releasing tension. I practiced making myself limp, then pushing and pulling against the floor with my feet and legs, hands and arms, to try to keep my whole body flexible.

Queenie came on duty again with her special friend "Princess," as I dubbed her. They spread out a stack of letters and began to work, and I soon realized they were trying to translate some correspondence written in English. They got stuck on the letters *l-a*. I couldn't figure out whether the word was "law" or what, and finally the teacher in me won out. I asked.

"Well, it's l-a," they said suspiciously.

"What's the next word?"

"S-a-l-l-e."

They had uncovered a letter from the La Salle Correspondence School and were trying to figure it out. I explained that "la" was part of the name "*La Salle.*"

It was a minor diversion, but it reassured me my mind was still alert. The longer I sat in that chair facing the wall, the more I wondered what would happen next. I was afraid we would run out of reading material, for I knew the students were already having difficulty finding more books. I had polished off more than two dozen by now, mostly novels, trying not to fly through them with my customary speed.

I was thinking about the other hostages all the time. How many of us were being held? Who else had been captured? I prayed for them daily, terribly concerned about the questioning that some of them might be going through and wondering how they were coping. Could I be of any help if I somehow got away? *There are some tall trees close to the compound wall. . . . Maybe I could climb one of those trees and get over the wall.*

I knew an Iranian family who lived close to the embassy.

Could I make it to their house? If I could just get them to loan me a chador and put me in a cab so that I could get away. . . . It would be very dangerous for anyone to help me, but still. . . . Is it a possibility?

The temptation to run grew stronger at night when all seemed quiet and I was sure the sister was falling asleep. But always she would stir, or at that moment when my courage was highest another sister would pop in to visit.

Certainly there must be something else I could do. And as I pondered it, the idea came to me: *You can pray. You can pray for a lot of things.*

I had wondered what it would be like to live in a contemplative community ever since I visited Mayerling, outside of Vienna. There are people there who spend their entire lives in prayer for the repose of the souls of the Prince of Austria and the woman he loved (they had died in a double murder-suicide). I was not a Catholic, but the idea of a contemplative life-style intrigued me. What would it be like? Here was my opportunity to find out.

I set up my morning's program. I decided to spend the early morning in special prayer, concentrating on a different topic each day. I chose Mondays as a day of prayer for the institutions of the churches. Tuesday I prayed for all of the various human crises in the world: for world hunger, for those who are oppressed, for those who are ill, and for all sorts of social needs. On Wednesday I prayed for my family and my friends, starting in one corner of the United States and praying through all of the different locations across the country.

I soon found out prayer was a lot more difficult than I had thought it would be. The difficulty was in running out of things to say. After asking God to bless Mom and Dad and to cure the evils of the world, what next?

After several days of struggling, I began to think more about focusing and concentrating on God: designing a worship ceremony, creating a liturgy, and setting up a regular routine of prayer. I was surprised at the amount of discipline it took to think in terms of being in God's presence.

I was crawling when I desperately wanted to run. But it was the beginning of truly learning about prayer. I built on what I already knew, using songs and hymns and verses from Scriptures I had memorized as a child. And surprisingly, after a while I was thinking in terms of thankfulness as well as petition.

I soon realized that praying was helping very much to ease my mind about my parents. I had had no word from them, but I assumed that the students were not letting us have any communication with the outside world. They had been so insistent that no one could speak to the Americans in the embassy when I was outside looking in, at the Ahnjoman. I was terribly concerned, but I knew my family was praying because we had always prayed. And they knew I would be praying for strength for them.

About the third day in the library, I spotted an Armed Forces Service Hymnal on a closet shelf. When I asked for it, the sister answered in surprise, "That's not a book to read."

"Please give it to me," I asked. "I'll show you what it is." And I explained to her the parts of the hymnal: the liturgy, the Scripture passages, and the hymns. When I finished, she simply handed me the book and walked away.

What a provision this was for my prayer time! I used the hymnal very sparingly in those early days, for I was afraid they would take it away from me. It contained many of the Psalms and numerous other Scripture readings, and it was filled with the hymns I had learned as a child—so much of which I could only remember in frustrating snatches, otherwise. It was a precious gift, and I guarded it carefully.

During this time I began to notice a guard who was giving haircuts to the other girls while she was on duty with me. Her name was Seroor. She taught mathematics in a girls' school in southern Tehran and was working on a master's degree at night. At twenty-four, she was clearly one of the important leaders of the young women.

Seroor had a very quiet way about her, and she seemed to be serious about doing whatever she could to relieve the plight of her fellowman. One day she came on duty with a beautiful new blouse and head scarf. And the next day, there she was, back again with her old, cotton print head scarf and an old blouse and sweater she had worn repeatedly. I said something about her new head scarf from the day before. She smiled and said, "Someone else needed it."

It was Seroor who one day arranged for me to go outside for just a few moments and stand on the front steps of the residence. I had not been outside since the first day I had been taken hostage.

It had rained the night before, so everything was damp. But the rain no doubt had been welcomed because of the long, hot, dry summer. The sun was shining brightly, the sky blue, and the air was clear and crisp, cool but not cold. To be outside and smell the clean, rain-fresh air and see the green! The feeling was indescribable.

I gazed across the green lawn still glistening with rain and abruptly realized the trees edging the grounds were much farther away from the compound wall than I had thought. There were brothers lounging with rifles at the corners of the buildings. My escape route was gone. Oh, well. There was no way I would have been able to climb one of those trees, anyway. The bottom branch was much too high for me.

Several leaves rustled across the ground in the breeze, and I picked up a gold one from the terrace and carried it inside. That little bit of outside carried in would become a part of my daily life for the next year, marking the place in my hymnbook for daily devotionals.

Relentlessly, slowly, the days moved on. It was December 6, 1979, my mother's birthday. Seroor was on duty so I asked, "May I have a piece of paper and a pencil? I'd like to write my mother."

"I don't know," said Seroor. "I'll have to find out."

"It's her birthday," I continued. "She'll be sixty-nine years old. I know she's terribly worried about me."

69

I knew the men were writing and sending letters, for when I was in the little house I had overheard one of them say, "Now, you send that letter to Germany. My wife is in Germany. I want her to know I'm all right," and the student had promised him that he would send it.

"I'll see. I'll ask if it's possible," I was told again.

It was possible. She returned with a pencil and a piece of paper.

I had not yet cried in captivity. I had been trained as a child that tears were no solution to a problem, and I was determined not to let these women see me let go. But as I wrote my parents, the tears began to slip silently down my cheeks.

Seroor looked at me. "Why are you crying?"

"It's very difficult *not* to cry. My parents and my family are all very important to me. This must be terribly hard on them, not knowing what's happening. All they know is that I've been kidnapped and taken hostage."

She continued to gaze at me quietly. "But you're *alive!* There are an awful lot of mothers in Tehran whose sons and daughters have been killed by the Shah."

I turned back to my writing, rather impatiently, and thought about what was going on at home. Mother and Daddy were probably in Washington with Mary Jane, or perhaps even in Florida for Christmas holidays with my sister Anabeth and her family by this time. Some of my other sisters would probably be there, and Mother would be getting phone calls from the others.

I probably would have called Mother from Iran if I had been in my own little house. We had always been very caring; and as the family scattered throughout the United States, we had become increasingly close. If we couldn't be together physically, we always made the effort to remember each other's birthdays and anniversaries and the holidays by sending cards and letters and using that wonderful instrument, the telephone. Not being able to be with the family in some way was hard.

I finished the letter, including birthday wishes for Mother and instructions about Christmas presents for my nieces and nephews, and gave it to Seroor. Later Miryam, one of the sisters, assured me she had mailed it.

The guard changed again, and then again. The girls casually threw their bags of knitting and books and sweaters on the empty bookshelves near my chair. Suddenly I noticed something glinting in the light among the wool and string bags and ragged papers. It was a little silver penknife, lying quite out in the open for me to see. Assuming we would be tied up again in the future, I decided to take the gamble. In a few minutes I stood up to stretch and managed to put the book I was reading on top of the knife. Was the guard looking? In one swift movement I picked up the book roughly, and the penknife was on the floor. Five more minutes and I had managed to slip the knife underneath the rug with my toe.

Later in the day one of the girls came back looking for her possession. On the one hand, I felt guilty not telling her where it was. But on the other, I knew that if the situation became desperate, I might need it.

I imagine the penknife is still there, safely hidden under the ambassador's rug, for that night three sisters came into the room and told me to get my things together. I had a toothbrush and some toothpaste, a comb, the hymnal, and the slacks and pullover from the co-op. I put on my cape and my blindfold obediently and was loaded into a car. The car went about three blocks and stopped. I climbed out into the crisp, cool air for only a moment, to be led inside again, down some steps and through what seemed to be a long, long corridor, up one flight of steps, then another. I knew I was on the second floor of the chancellery.

We took a turn and walked and walked. Finally, forty-two steps later, I passed through a doorway and heard the door shut behind me. I was led across the room, lowered in a chair, and my blindfold taken off.

I was in a room I'd never seen before: very small, about

ten by twelve, with bookcases lining two walls. It was the political library of the embassy, filled with all sorts of interesting books. My eyes quickly flitted over the titles. There were old books, books about Iran, and some very practical volumes like *Who's Who*, a big dictionary, and a collection of Persian art books. It was a wide variety in subject matter, but all the books dealt with ancient Persia, modern Iran, and the Middle East. It looked like a great place to be. *At least I'll be able to read!* I thought.

There was a desk in one corner of the room, a typing table and a typing chair for the sister to sit on, and a heater with the plug missing. I watched rather apprehensively as the sisters twisted the exposed wires of the heater and poked them into the wall outlet. Playing with electricity was one game I was terrified of, and I didn't relish the idea of sitting in darkness because of a blown fuse.

For the first time since I'd been moved out of the little house, a brother brought a mattress. So now I had a mattress, a blanket, *and* a pillow. I was almost more comfortable here than I had been in the little house.

Morning brought more new discoveries, good and bad. I soon realized my new room was right next to the vault. Thus began days and nights of a constant banging of the heavy vault door: banging open, banging shut. One new headache.

I also discovered that I was right across from the toilet, a facility being used by other American hostages. How good it was to hear those distinctive American voices! Somebody else was around. Somebody else was fighting back, and somebody else was carrying on and doing all right. But how frustrating, when things obviously *weren't* all right, that there was no way I could reach out to help that someone.

Those morning and evening sounds of voices proved to be a refuge from the enemy outside. The windows in the political library were too high for me to see anything but a few treetops and blessed blue sky. But I could hear the crowds more clearly than ever, which made me very much aware how close to the street I was here.

There was a bullet hole in one of the windows, left over from the February take-over of the embassy. And the sounds outside the embassy were nerve-wracking, bringing back my fears in full force: fear that someone would come in and take me off for questioning or a trial; fear that the students would turn on me; but most of all, fear that the mobs outside would somehow break loose, go out of control, and come over the embassy wall.

Having seen the "camp out" lines of Iranians waiting for exit permits, visas, and other papers before the take-over, I could easily visualize the households that had been set up in the streets in front of the embassy. There seemed to be a continuous crowd of people shouting anti-American slogans, listening to the exhortations of the students and mullahs* who were always on hand. In addition to the crowd noises, there were three or four loudspeakers blaring newscasts in Farsi—too distorted to understand—replays of the student demands, music that had been developed for the revolution, and yesterday's political harangue. And through it all I could almost hear the sounds of Coke, kabob, and candy vendors. The racket was not unlike a Mad Hatters' carnival or a football game gone berserk. I had the distinct feeling *I* was the football!

One morning in particular the noise felt like needles, penetrating that small room. As I sat confined in my chair I thought, *I can't take this. I just can't take this.* One anti-American protest song, probably from the Vietnam War era, was being played endlessly, and it cut like a knife through my head. "Dear Lord," I prayed, "I'm afraid I can't take this. Help me. Give me some of that peace that passes all understanding."

I was so tense, I thought I would fly into a million pieces. But resolutely I began to go through my morning prayer list. A little later I became conscious of the fact that while the

---

* A Muslim clergyman.

noise hadn't abated one decible, I was at peace. Another gift from the Lord.

The hoarse chanting (it almost sounded like a Marine sound-off, there were so many low-pitched, male voices) didn't go away, however, and I could vividly imagine the leers of hatred on the faces of the mob. The scene began at 6:00 each morning and did not stop until 2:00 A.M. the next day. Fridays were particularly bad, for that was the day people came for prayers.

I was afraid my initial assessment was going to be right. It might be six months before we were released. I knew the Shah was a sick man, and so I did not expect him to live much beyond that time. And if he was not alive, what would be the purpose of holding us? "Dear God, *please* let this be settled," I prayed again and again.

I decided that even if I couldn't go home, perhaps I could write another letter. I could only hope the first one had reached my family. I still had not received any word from them. I wondered if they would be permitted to write me. I wrote my letter and returned to reading, though not the dusty volumes around me. They were forbidden as "spy books."

Queenie had a second try at interrogation. She was on duty, translating more letters at the typing table, when she started a "conversation" about my work. We spoke in Farsi now, because I hoped to improve my facility in the language while I was in this situation. She asked about the activities I pursued during the course of my work; I told her extensively about the things we had done when I had served at the American Cultural Center in Zambia, and how we were trying to reorganize the Cultural Center in Tehran.

During the course of the conversation she started talking about the press. "How do you relate to them?" she asked. As we continued talking she began taking notes and writing down very carefully what was being said, surreptitiously behind the stack of letters she was translating. My antenna began to wave.

74

"Hahnum," I said, still in Farsi, "when you were just talking about reporters, you were talking about Iranian reporters who came to me to find out about American things, weren't you?"

"No, I was talking about foreign reporters talking to you about Iran and what was happening here. People who were reporting to you!" she added triumphantly.

"Sorry, sister. I misunderstood you. I don't talk to that many foreign reporters (meaning reporters from outside Iran), and I certainly wouldn't be talking to them about what was going on here in Iran except as it might concern how we live, the cost of things, or what the Iran-American Society does."

"Oh . . . I see."

Even as Queenie tried to be the sophisticated interrogator, she displayed naiveté about my work and what I was capable of doing. I am still convinced she used my lack of fluency to try and create a brilliant coup for herself in what my role in the embassy was. I never answered any more "technical" questions in Farsi after that.

In one of our more friendly moments, she asked me to translate words for her. She was doing some basic translation of letters and couldn't always read the handwriting.

"Miss Koob, what is c-l-o-v-e?" she asked, spelling it out. I told her it was a spice. She asked if there was another meaning as that didn't make sense in her letter.

"Could it be dove?" I asked, spelling it out. "A dove is a bird."

"Yes, that's it. How did you know that that was the word?" she asked.

I smiled. "I was a teacher for a while in Iowa, and I often had to read handwriting that wasn't perfect."

Those fleeting moments were almost pleasant. I enjoyed trying to guess which word was really intended, and sometimes I could read the back of the sheet of paper the students were working on. One letter said, "When you became a diplomat we were all so proud, and now this thing has . . ."

GUEST OF THE REVOLUTION

Obviously, the letter had been addressed to one of my colleagues, but even as Queenie was working on this letter, she assured me that the letters she was translating were written to the students. Many of them were. I could tell from the number of words I helped her translate what the general gist of some letters were, and I don't know how often I heard the oft-repeated "revenge" or "vengeance," which when coupled with other words I knew could only be related to appeals to the students for our release. I also saw them handle numerous cables, some of them with long lists of names.

Each cockeyed day seemed like the one before—distorted and out of focus. Occasionally, I was reassured by an American voice in the hall. But I could always hear street noises, and I never knew what the sisters would have to say. I added more strenuous exercise—running in place and toe touches—to my routine of prayer, contemplation, and reading, and wondered when the spectators would go home and the game would be over. On particularly frustrating days I ran, hard, an extra one hundred steps in place. I'd been in the arena quite long enough!

**Religious faith sustains
former Iowan during captivity,
her family says**
Des Moines Register
December 30, 1979

6

CHRISTMAS, 1979

Yuletide was approaching. We had been held well over a month. I was quite sure the situation would not be resolved in time for us to go home, but I kept praying it would be. This year wouldn't be the first Christmas I'd spent away from my family, but it certainly had all of the earmarks of being the strangest.

As December 25 grew closer and closer, I began to get signals from the sisters that they were aware this holiday was important to us. They started talking about the previous year, how the Christians in Iran had supported the revolution by not having Christmas trees, big parties, and gift exchanges. Instead, Christmas was kept as a purely religious festival.

My ears were working overtime during these days, straining to hear a sound that was never heard: a familiar Christmas melody. Every day I sorted through the clamor outside my window, yearning to hear one acknowledgment of Christmas by the Islamic Republic to its Christian constituents. But there was only the din of hatred, the anti-American slogans, and the rhetoric of the Islamic revolution.

Through the blare of the multiple loudspeakers, set at ear-splitting levels, I could hear occasional snatches of mu-

77

sic, even a solitary violin melody. But day in and day out, the overwhelming theme was the continuous sloganeering and the chanting of the students, always culminating in the call for death.

I spent hours thinking about the paradox of preparing for the coming of the Prince of Peace while being surrounded by—and being the object of—so much hatred. Reconciling the truths I had been taught about forgiveness and love in Christ with the violence and calls for execution that surrounded me now proved difficult.

Determinedly, I lingered on themes of peace, love, and understanding as I prayed for patience, courage, and strength to meet each day. At night my pillow was often wet from tears as I thought about my family—my sisters, their husbands and children, and my parents. I knew that Christmas would be different for them because I was a prisoner, but I was also confident their faith in the power of God and His love was strong. They would not let what had happened to me turn this time of celebration into days of mourning and self-pity.

My favorite fantasy was of being released in time to get to the States, do some last-minute shopping, and then fly to Anabeth's to be with the clan. I made mental gift lists for everyone, but more than anything I wanted to buy blue mother-daughter robes for Anabeth and my niece Emma Lou.

I wrote another letter home in late December and mentioned that friends really would think I was awful for not sending Christmas cards two years in a row. The year before, I had returned from Zambia in August, but my household goods had not arrived until December; and with all the unpacking, I never had gotten my Christmas cards written.

Since cards seemed to be out of the question this year, I was determined to do something special for each person who would have been on that list: I prayed for each one, asking the Lord's special blessing for them during the season.

During this time I began to learn about joy. I couldn't pray for a happy or fun-filled Christmas for my family, but I could and did ask the Lord to fill them with the quiet joy of peace and love that was embodied in the first coming of our Savior. I didn't realize it then, but I was learning to distinguish between "joy" and "glee." Real joy, I would come to see, shines through sorrow, pain, and grief. What a beautiful gift!

I had been following my "contemplative order" for only a few weeks, and each day brought something new to think about. But Christmas was coming. In the midst of all this turmoil, the day of the celebration of Christ's birth was drawing closer and closer.

Time and time again, I verified the date in order to create my own calendar, counting back from Christmas to determine the first Sunday of Advent. All too soon it was time to open my hymnal to the Advent section, a rich source of prayers and hymns. I was determined not to use Christmas carols until two weeks before Christmas.

I still had no Bible, so I tried to recall from memory the scriptural prophecies of the incarnation of the Son of God. Remembering general ideas was easy, but recalling entire biblical passages was much more frustrating. I knew bits of the prophecy from Genesis—the promise that the woman would conceive and bear a Son and the Son would overpower Satan. I could also remember snatches from Isaiah, ". . . and his name shall be called Wonderful, Counselor, The mighty God, The everlasting Father, The Prince of Peace." And from Micah: "Thou, Bethlehem Ephratah, though thou be little among the thousands of Judah, yet out of thee shall he come forth unto me that is to be ruler in Israel." But I didn't know all the words and thus couldn't recite the verses correctly.

Finally the reality settled in that even the fastest plane wouldn't get us home for Christmas. Reluctantly I gave up the mental shopping spree, the reunion with the family, and worship at home for Christmas, 1979. I would find out if Christmas was really what I had always claimed: the celebration of the birth of the Savior.

My deadline came and went, and I began to sing those

79

beloved Christmas carols, humming then inaudibly to myself or singing them quietly while snuggled down in my blanket in the big easy chair in my corner of the library.

I discovered new meaning in many of these old friends, the hymns. The third verse of "It Came Upon a Midnight Clear" was a good example. The hymn had never been a favorite, but now the words had such special meaning.

> *And you, beneath life's crushing load,*
> *Whose forms are bending low,*
> *Who toil along the climbing way*
> *With painful steps and slow:*
> *Look now, for glad and golden hours*
> *Come swiftly on the wing;*
> *Oh, rest beside the weary road*
> *And hear the angels sing!*

Christmas Eve morning arrived. As usual, I was restricted to my big chair in the political library of the American Embassy. With the Armed Forces Service Hymnal at my side and my mind still straining to remember the promises from Micah, Genesis, and Isaiah in full, I continued my daily worship.

The girls were much aware it was almost Christmas. Besides the guard on duty, a number of them flitted in and out to talk. My first order of the day was to ask if we Americans would be able to have a minister and a worship service. I used the word "priest," because that was the only Farsi word I knew for minister. I talked with them about how important Christmas worship was to me and how I had always gone to church on Christmas Eve, no matter where I was in the world.

The girls exhibited much curiosity about Christmas: What was special about it? Did we have special food? Why did we go to church? What did we do at our house? What about Christmas trees? And presents? Was it time for being together with family?

I talked about what had happened at our home when I was growing up on the farm in Iowa. I was the oldest of six girls, and yes, we always had a tree. I talked about Daddy putting the lights on the tree and then all of us taking turns adding our favorite ornaments one by one. I told about how we saved them from year to year and that they were in some respects a history of our family.

As I talked to the girls, I could visualize all of us sisters as children again. I was the bookworm. My second sister, Micki, was the artist and designer. Vivian was the outdoor girl and loved to drive the tractor, help Daddy, and work hard on the farm.

Anabeth, sister number four, was the homebody and the "responsible one," according to my parents. How that irked the rest of us sometimes! She would see it was time to get the cows without having to be told, or she would feed the chickens when it was her turn to do so, not having to be reminded.

Mary Jane was the quiet one. She could spend hours by herself wandering about, thinking, reading, singing, talking; and Emi, the "baby," was pert and vivacious, and extremely popular with all of her friends.

How different we all were, and yet how we all loved Grandmother's *lebkuchen* (German Christmas cookies), which were made at the beginning of Advent, and the dozens of various kinds of goodies we made in preparation for the Christmas holidays. I stopped to explain to the sisters how Christmas actually started with the four weeks of Advent, the time we prepare to commemorate the coming to earth of Jesus Christ, and compared it to the preparation time that was used during the Islamic month of Ramadan. The analogy was not exactly appropriate, but the girls did understand preparation and waiting.

I mentioned the special Bible passages that were read about the coming of our Lord and Savior during church services on the Sundays of Advent, and I described the Advent wreaths we always made at home. I realized again what this Christmas would be like: alone in my room, no letters from home, no opportunity to be with my family in any way, except through prayer.

I soon began to understand that the sisters were pumping me for information. My first inkling of what was going on came at about 5:30 that afternoon. The door opened, and a masculine hand thrust a branch of a plastic Christmas tree into the room. Someone in the hall asked, "Does she want a tree?"

"I'd be delighted," I volunteered.

So, into the room the branch came. It looked like a lower branch of a large, synthetic tree, but it could be stood upright. I searched the room and, oddly enough, found the base to a flag pole. It made a dandy tree stand.

Next came some rather gaudy decorations. I didn't want those on *my* tree. Some pink routing slips were lying on top of the desk, so I tore them into strips and with bits of Scotch tape, made a pink chain to put on the bottom of the tree. There was also white paper and brown paper, so I started folding and, after some mishaps, I remembered how in school days we had made snowflakes to decorate our classroom windows.

At that point the student who was on duty became fascinated with what I was doing. I showed her how to fold the paper, and she very busily made a few more snowflakes to add to the collection. Then, one of my experiments turned out to be a little cross, which I put on the top of the tree.

I looked at it all and thought, *No Christmas tree is complete without a manger scene.* Thinking back to my experience as a district parish worker for the American Lutheran Church, I picked up some more paper and began to fold again. Before too long, I had a fairly acceptable representation of the Virgin Mary, Joseph, and with a little more manipulation, a manger and a tiny bundle to lay inside to represent the Christ Child. A little more thought, and after a couple of attempts that didn't turn out quite so well, I finally had an angel. He stood behind Mary and Joseph, taller than both of them, with his wings spread protectively over them as they knelt, looking at the little crib with the bundle of the Christ Child. I now had a crèche under the Christmas tree.

Just as we finished up there was the usual changing of

the guard. This brought about another discussion in regard to the crêche. "Who is that? What do they represent?" And when I talked abut the figures representing Mary and Joseph and the Christ Child. . . "Well, who's Joseph?"

Patiently I explained that Joseph was Mary's husband, not the father of Christ but the man who took Mary as his wife. This explanation began a rather detailed discussion about the fact that, in Islam, Mary, or Maryam as she is called in the Koran, did not have a husband, ever. She actually had a protector, an older man, probably Zechariah, the father of John the Baptist. Finally I said, "Well, that may be in the Koran, but in the Bible there's a Joseph, and he's very important."

Among the decorations that the students thrust through the door (and they didn't all come at once) was a tinsel star. Because I already had made my little cross for the top of the tree, I took the tinsel star and hung it on a lower branch, right over the crêche, a star over the place where Christ lay.

A little later, another hand came in through the door, and a voice said, "Would she like a Bible?"

Would I like a Bible! How precious. Before the sister had a chance to repeat the question, I had answered in a loud voice, "Yes, she'd like a Bible!" A King James Bible found its way into the room. I inspected the volume hopefully for clues as to its owner and found nothing. But it didn't matter. I had the Holy Scriptures! This Bible was to be my companion through the many, many months that lay ahead.

A little later in the evening, about 10:00 P.M., several of the brothers came with a box full of Christmas cards. "You may write two," one of them said. I looked through the box carefully and selected one for my family and one for my dear friend Milton in Zambia. To be able to write a letter! I did hope they would send it. I had no inkling it would be the first letter my family received.

The brother also asked if there was anything I needed. Evidently the Ayatollah had said we could have whatever we wanted that night.

"Yes, I would like a sheet, some nylons, and my face cream." They brought a sheet very quickly, and some face cream, but finding stockings in my size proved hopeless.

I wrote my family on that Christmas Eve: "Almost every year of my life I have received a book for Christmas, and this one was no different. But this year, I received the Book of Books—the Holy Bible." It was almost too much. I could scarely do anything but sit and hold that precious volume.

When I finished my two cards, the guard—the third one that evening—asked me what I had said. I briefly translated what I had written, and when she left she took the letters with her. I breathed a prayer that they would be mailed.

I had my Christmas tree, I had a crêche, and I had the Bible. Word seemed to have spread about my decorations, for there were more girls than usual dropping by to visit the guard. They were eager to ask more questions about Christmas. "Don't you miss your family? Would you be with your family? What would you have to eat? What would you be doing?"

So I talked again about Christmas. "If I were at home in Iowa, my family would have an early dinner, probably oyster stew, and then we would go to church, where the Sunday school children would tell the story of the birth of Jesus through hymns, Scripture prophecies, and recitations."

I had often wondered how Christmas would be without tinsel, without lots of goodies, without weeks of preparation in the kitchen. No presents to wrap, none to buy. Like many people, I claimed Christmas was the celebration of the birth of the Christ Child and I didn't need those things. But did I?

As I strained for the sound of Christmas through the noise outside my window, I thought I heard the bells of Christmas ringing at 11:00 P.M. They were calling the faithful to worship at the church located diagonally across the way from the entrance to the ambassador's residence.

I set about creating my own worship. A carol, "O Come, O Come, Emmanuel." The prophecies from Genesis and Micah. "O Little Town of Bethlehem." And where in Isaiah was the verse with the words "Wonderful, Counselor, Mighty God, Prince of Peace"? Carefully I searched. There it was: Isaiah 9:6. "For unto us a child is born. . . ."

In the middle of noise and turmoil, Christ was born; and in the middle of all this noise and turmoil, I could celebrate anew. What a graphic example of His coming into the world to bring peace. I thought of the peace that had come when I needed it and how Christ had come when we needed Him. And my mind leaped forward to the scene at Pontius Pilate's palace. I could understand now much more clearly the scene of the crowd demanding the death of Christ. "Crucify Him! Crucify Him!" was echoed here each day with *"Marg bar Cartare"* and *"Marg bar Ahm-ri-ka."* Each day I listened to cries for death. I could see through Christmas to Lent and Good Friday. Christ's love had come to live among us at Christmas, not denying the agony of the Cross.

I read the story of the Annunciation in Matthew and then turned to Luke 2 to read the old familiar story. One by one I sang the hymns: "While Shepherds Watched Their Flocks by Night," "Angels We Have Heard on High," and finally "Silent Night."

The guard was watching and interrupted me to ask about the hymns. "What are those marks? Do you know how to read them? What do the hymns say?" I explained as best I could.

Christmas Eve in Tehran. I *could* kneel in solitude at the manger of the Christ Child and celebrate. The message that Christ had come to mankind was the only reason to celebrate. Filled with fright for the situation and longing for my family, but confident in the love of the Father, I prepared my room for sleeping.

The guard changed again. It was Queenie with a plate of goodies—nuts, brownies, cookies, caramels, and an orange. I ate one cookie and put the rest aside. "Why don't you eat them all?" she asked.

"I'm saving some for tomorrow."

"Isn't it like what you have at home?" she asked smugly.

"Yes. But we don't eat it all on Christmas Eve," I replied. "We save some for later. If I ate them all, I would be sick. Here, please have some."

"No, it's for you," she said, still proud of herself.

"Christmas gifts aren't much good if they can't be shared. Please, have some." I offered the plate again.

She looked amazed at my statement, carefully selected the smallest piece, said thank you, and ate it.

I snuggled with my head down under the blanket that night, with just a corner of my cover open so I could see my crèche with the star hanging over it. I prayed for God to bless my family and to give them a joyful Christmas.

A little later, I was awakened by someone gently shaking my shoulder. "Hahnum Koob, get dressed," said Seroor. "They're waiting for you. A priest is here."

Completely disoriented, I stumbled out of my makeshift bed and into my dress and my cape. Gently she blindfolded me and then guided me out of the chancellery and across the courtyard. I was still trying to clear my head of sleep, and I was so nervous I could hardly move. Suddenly my blindfold was whipped off, and I went inside.

We were in the commercial library, just around the corner from the USICA offices. In a split second I saw that the walls were completely lined with slogans, pictures of Khomeini, horrible picures of war, and thirty or forty students, mostly male, gaping at me from the crowded corners of the room. "I will not give them the satisfaction of reading their slogans. I will focus only on the Prince," I muttered angrily, steeling myself against the bright lights.

Then I saw the large Christmas tree, a table filled with Christmas goodies, and Ann Swift. There were also two ministers, robed in white, with stoles. There was a candle, and a chalice—*Communion!* What a Christmas present! I hugged Ann and asked her how she was and explained to the priest that we hadn't seen each other for over a month.

One of the ministers shook hands with us and said, "I'm Bishop Gumbleton from Detroit. We just had Mass with some of the men. We'd like to have a service with you." He continued, "We'll not have a full Mass, but we will have a worship service. Would you like to take Communion?"

"If it is permitted."

He said gently, "Of course."

Ann said she would like Communion, too. He began to lead us in a worship service, and during that time, we had a chance to pray aloud. I scarcely knew how to begin, except to pray that our families would know we were all right. And I prayed that there would be a resolution to the conflict. Ann told me later it was a beautiful prayer. I didn't remember a word of it.

I was in a complete state of shock. My whole body was trembling so violently I had to use every power of concentration I had ever developed in acting classes to keep myself under rigid control. This time with Ann and Father Gumbleton was too precious, too important, for me to fall apart. To keep myself under tight rein, I doubled my fist until my nails cut deeply into my hands, and I forced my knees to be absolutely still. I wanted Father Gumbleton to be able to go home and tell the folks I was all right and that I was doing well. I never saw the television cameras the students had set up so meticulously.

After the worship service, we were offered soft drinks, fruit, and sweets from the table, gaily decorated with red tablecloths and the unmistakable sight of Coca-Cola bottles. At this point, the second minister was introduced to us by someone, and we were told that he was a cardinal from Algeria. He did not speak English, but because Ann and I understood French, he spoke to us and asked how many Catholics there were in Tehran. In my faulty French I replied that I didn't know, because I was a Lutheran, and Ann said she was Episcopalian. This he found extremely amusing, but the warmth of his handshake and the strength of his embrace did not diminish. We were, after all, fellow Christians facing a trying time.

I asked if they had brought devotional material for us, and Bishop Gumbleton gave his lectionary to me. He told the students it was given to the two of us, and that we were both to use it. The students promised this would be seen to. Then, we were told it was time to go. Hoping to prolong the visit a little bit, I said, "Let's sing some carols." We stood, and as we were being blindfolded, Ann and I started singing. Bishop Gumbleton joined us. We managed "Joy to the World" and "Hark, the Herald Angels Sing" before we left the room. Ann was singing "Silent Night" when I last heard her voice.

Seroor led me back to my room. For the second time I snuggled down into my blanket. I wasn't really sure the whole episode had happened.

As I arranged my covers, Seroor sat down on the floor beside my bed. My feelings finally caught up with me and I really let go. What had I said? Why didn't I say more? I was trembling in the aftermath of the shock.

Seroor must have sensed my emotional state, for quietly she asked if I had liked the service. I told her I had and asked if the priest could please visit once more before he left. She was noncommittal.

"What do you really want for Christmas?" she asked instead.

"I suppose for this conflict to be settled peacefully so we can *all* go home," I replied. I looked at her steadily. "What do you want?"

"I want so much for my country." She spoke even more softly. There were tears in her eyes. "I want roads, and more schools for girls, clinics and hospitals."

It was a quiet moment.

"I hope you get them," I said, and I meant it. Seroor was one of the students who was sincerely working hard for her dreams to become realities. I knew she was teaching in a depressed area. I had seen her give away what few material possessions she had, and I truly wanted her to see her dreams realized.

When I woke on Christmas Day, I knew the service had been real, for there, beside my bed where I had put it the night before, was the red-bound lectionary from Bishop Gumbleton. The Bible the students had given me the night before was beside it, and under the tree stood the crèche with the star—the star of hope—shining brightly above it.

Christmas Day was in some ways anticlimactic.

I acquired my own table knife, fork, and dinner-sized plate that day, which had been an on-again, off-again problem from the first day. And there was a lovely dinner: roast turkey, stuffing, pies, cakes, and the most beautiful thing of all—garnishes of real, crisp, raw celery! It was all I could do to refrain from grabbing it all at once. But I took only two pieces and ate them slowly, savoring every crunchy, flavorful bite.

The priests were not allowed to visit us. I sat for much of the day simply holding the Bible and the lectionary, which I sent off to Ann that evening, as agreed.

During our conversation the night before I had described making a crèche and having it under my tree. Ann said she didn't have one, so on Christmas morning I started making another. Immediately the guards and their friends wanted to know about it.

"This one is for Miss Swift," I said.

"Oh, she has one," the girls said immediately.

"She told me last night she didn't have one," I replied evenly. "I wonder if she made one."

"Yes, she did," I was informed.

"Well, please see if you can give this one to her," I asked.

They took it away finally, and I did learn eventually that she received it. But the students let us pass the lectionary back and forth only three days before they informed me that Ann had received one of her own. That, I knew instinctively, was an outright lie.

Christmas in a strange land. Christmas as a hostage. But it *was* Christmas: the promise of the Old Testament fulfilled in the present, the birth of the Prince of Peace and a chance to celebrate His presence among us.

**Six U.S. envoys escape Iran/Friendly
embassies had sheltered them**
Des Moines Register
January 29, 1980

7

JANUARY, 1980

The days following Christmas were quiet and depressing. The Christmas tree stood faithfully in the corner. I had my Bible and Bishop Gumbleton's lectionary. The holidays had passed, but the sisters still had questions: "Was it a good celebration?" "Did you like the food?"

I finally asked them a question of my own: "What about the mail? I saw bags of mail at the Christmas celebration. Isn't there any for me?"

To my surprise, the brothers arrived with a large plastic sack, and I was allowed to pull four cards out. One was from a family in Iowa! "Give the cards to the sisters when you have read them," they instructed. "They will give them back to you if you want." I held those cards in my hands, read and reread the messages, and caressed them over and over again. How good it was to have mail from home.

The days passed slowly. I was given a man's short wool dressing gown, which meant I no longer had to sleep in my dress or slacks. My sleep improved considerably. I could change at night, leaving my daytime clothes close by my eyeglasses and Bible, ready to go in case I should have to move again quickly.

Mornings I slept late, until about 10:00, a decided luxury for me. Then my routine was to grab my toothbrush, go across the hall, wash, brush my teeth, and get ready for the day.

The second day I had the dressing gown, the sister stopped me in midstep. "No. You can't go to the bathroom dressed like that."

"The brother gave it to me," I replied. "It's what they want me to wear. If he doesn't like it, he can turn around and not look."

She shook her head. "No. How about your coat?"

I shook my head. "You washed that and it shrunk." They had tossed the wool cape my grandmother had made me into the washer without asking.

Then I had a bright idea. "How about this?" I said, pulling up a blanket and wrapping it around me sarong style. We were both happy. I was covered, and her sense of modesty was no longer offended. This way, I could wash up before putting on my daytime clothes.

I took a few minutes each morning to set the room to rights. I stood the mattress against the wall, folded the blankets and sheets, and settled into my chair. I was ready for my opening morning prayer, which had evolved to: "Thank You, Lord, for bringing me safely through the night. Thank You for today. I give it back to You. Show me what You would have me do. Amen."

I decided to start reading six chapters in the Old Testament, a bit from the Book of Psalms, two chapters from the Gospels, and two chapters from the Epistles. I underlined passages that particularly struck me at the time with a stub of a pencil I had found in the depths of my chair.

After my morning meditations I found it hard to keep from thinking about my family and friends: recent friends, old friends, friends who went back to my early childhood; the things we had done together. I thought of the plays I had directed when I was teaching high school in Newton, Iowa, and the three summers I had spent at the University of Denver working on my Master's degree in theater. All those

91

people who had been important to me. How I missed them! What were they doing now? Did they know about me?

I snuggled into the corner of my chair, and for a moment, if I closed my eyes, I could imagine that it was my friend Milton who was holding me and that I was safe again. He had been a very special part of my life while I was in Zambia for three years, my last overseas assignment. My thoughts drifted back to sitting on the banks of the Luangua River, watching the herds of elephants come down to drink. I remembered one fresh morning out in the bush so clearly. I came out of my tent and looked up and saw the parade of elephants across the skyline. Then came the antelope, the water buffalo, and a family of chimpanzees, down to the riverbank to wash themselves and to drink. All those wonderful memories. All my friends. *But how will I remember Iran?*

I continued to mark the hours by the snatches of radio I heard, but I had also learned to tell time by the movement of the shadows and sunlight from one side of the room to the other. I wasn't sure how I felt as I watched the last rays of the sun change color and finally disappear from the faces of the stacked oak book cases and rough, cream-colored plastered walls. Methodically I listened for the snap of the drapery hooks as one of the sisters whipped the drapes across the traverse rods. Another day was done, one day closer to "the end of captivity."

When had that phrase become a reality? I couldn't remember. But I was aware that as each day was completed, we were one day nearer to the end. I could not project when that end would be.

January 1, 1980, was the roughest day of the whole ordeal. I never have been able to identify exactly why. It was simply the most depressing and discouraging day I had while in captivity. Nothing special happened, but I was absolutely blue.

At mid-morning someone knocked at the door. In a flurry

of chador the sister went to see who was there. Another of the sisters entered bearing a homemade New Year's hat and a card from Ann. It brightened my spirits some. I never would have thought of putting together a hat. *I don't like New Year's Eve parties*, I thought negatively, *but it would have been nice to get together with friends.*

I watched the sun's rays warm the walls, first on one side of the room, and then on the other. Another day was gone, a downer. Silently I wondered what the New Year would bring.

I woke up on January 2 feeling a bit better. The sun was hitting the 9:30 A.M. mark on the bookcase to my right, so I closed my eyes for a few more minutes. That day passed routinely. And the next.

On January 4, mid-morning, I took a notion to write. I had written a letter on Christmas Eve, ten days ago. Could I get permission to write another one? I asked the sisters to check with one of the brothers. Yes, it was possible. So I wrote to Mary Jane, finishing my Christmas story and asking for some tights. Then, shortly after I had finished, a brother appeared with three letters, all addressed to me!

Two were from my sister Micki, and one was from a childhood friend, Dorothy. I opened Dorothy's first. What incredible encouragement. It was absolutely filled with the love of the Holy Spirit, prayers for my well-being, and Scripture reference upon Scripture reference. I raced through the letter, my eyes blurring with tears, and then through the passages from the Bible: Isaiah, 1 Timothy, Romans. What love and care had gone into the composition of that letter!

As I started to open the letters from Micki—was I hearing right?—the brother announced, "When you have finished reading the letters give them to the sister. She will keep them for you." I had not even realized he was still in the room.

"What if I want to reread them?" I asked.

"She'll get them for you."

Think! Don't read them too fast, I cautioned myself. Should I let these precious links with my friend and family slip out of my hands? Not if I could help it! Watching the sister carefully, I tucked Dorothy's letter down beside the cushion on the chair, next to two pencils I had found. Slowly I opened the first of Micki's letters. As I did, I noted by the shadows that it was almost time to change guards. Maybe I could manage to keep these after all.

The first from Micki was a Thanksgiving card. Its message was short: love and prayers and a wonderfully amusing story about our niece, Carrie, and rabbit soup.

It seems Emi's girls, Suzie, Carrie, and Diann, had been given some rabbits. Their dad, teasing them, said, "I guess we'll have to make rabbit stew."

Carrie, age four, said, "I know how to make that!"

"You do!" said Emi. "How?"

"Well, you take a big pot of water and put it on the stove. You let it boil. Then you cut up a whole bunch of carrots and cook them and feed it to the rabbit."

For a moment, I was transported out of Tehran, across the Atlantic and into the Midwest, all the way to my sister's warm and comfortable kitchen. I was surrounded by the love of those three little girls, and I was *not* going to give up that letter. Inside the cover of my Bible it went!

The other letter from Micki assured me Mother and Daddy were all right. They were worried that I was worried about them. Micki reassured me she and my other sisters would do everything they could for them, and I knew they would.

The guard was changing. I listened closely. Nothing was said about the letters. I kept all of them!

Eventually the small amount of censored mail I was permitted to receive was delivered without instructions to give it back. What a comfort. Mail had been important to me at every overseas post, and here it was doubly precious. I had contact, however brief, with what was going on in the world of freedom.

The following day some of the sisters asked how long the celebration of Christmas lasted. "Until January 6," I told them, and tried to describe Epiphany. It seemed ironic that I would be explaining the visit of the Magi to people living in what many scholars believe was the home of the Magi, ancient Persia. But here was one more chance to share a bit of what I believed.

Queenie still thought herself in charge, and she and the others began to press their questioning and note-taking a bit further. One of the girls asked me pointedly: "Have you been questioned yet?"

"Of course," I said. "When I first came."

"No," she said, "I mean here."

"No." I tried to give the appearance of being cool and calm. "Not here. Why would they question me again? I told them everything during my first days here."

My mind was racing with the fear of what might happen. Where would they take me? What kind of games might they play? Would they ask me things about which I knew nothing? And would they believe me if I said I knew nothing?

Then it came. A sister arrived at 10:30 that evening and announced, "Hahnum, you are going to be moved. They want to question you."

Where am I going? I wondered. The girls in the room were full of disturbing giggles and side-long glances. Trying not to give away my anxiety, I gathered my things together again and wrapped them in my shrunken cape.

"Should we move the Christmas tree?" the girls asked.

"No," I said. "Today is January 5. I was going to take it down tomorrow." I took the paper snow flakes from it and left the candle, the star, and the crèche behind. They wouldn't pack too well.

Once more the girls tied my blindfold in place. My stuffed cape was in one hand and my Bible with those precious letters tucked inside in the other. Out the door we went, all of ten steps across the hall to what I saw when the blindfold was removed was another office.

I had never been in this room either. There was a large government issue wooden desk in the corner, turned around so that one could not open the drawers, a typing table, and three bookcases, for some reason also facing the wall. My

95

chair was brought into the room, as was the heater. I caught a glimpse of the windows before the sisters pulled the heavy draperies. Like the rest of the windows at the chancellery, they were waist high and very tall, about eight feet. But for security purposes they had been built up long ago to above the level of one's head with carefully secured and attractively painted metal boxes filled with sand, dirt, and gravel, thus preventing anyone inside from being shot by snipers. One of the windows was covered with blotting paper where a pane was missing.

Thump! A brother carelessly plopped my mattress on the floor, followed by the blankets and my pillow. I was "home." I put my toothbrush and comb in the drawer of the typing table. Later, I checked the recesses of my chair: The pencils were still there.

A further study of my new habitat revealed no writing on the walls. There was an adjoining door to the next office, but it was tightly shut. I could stand the mattress against the bookcases, I decided, which would mean more room to exercise. Having been moved to the other side of the building, I was sure I would be able to see the mountains when the sun shone in the morning. Best of all, there would be much less street noise here.

I counted my blessings that night as I settled down. As I prayed, I thought I heard someone next door. I listened carefully. Sure enough, it sounded like Mike Metrinko, one of the men from the political section of the embassy, talking to his guard in Farsi.

I was delighted to hear his voice. How I longed that my sister and his brother would leave our rooms at the same time. Then I could knock on the adjoining door, and he'd open the door and we'd both say, "Hi! How are you?" The others' well being was always uppermost in my mind. Or what would Mike think if both the guards fell asleep at the same time and I slipped in next door to talk?

It gave me a great sense of courage to know that Mike was still able to laugh and carry on with his guard. I knew he was fluent in Farsi, so the conversation was too rapid and muffled for me to understand much. But when I carefully rearranged my bed so the wind would not blow across me from the broken window, I ended up with my head on the pillow near the door between our rooms. I could see the light under the door and hear the conversation a little better.

Mike asked if the light could be turned off, and the glow under the door quickly faded from the brilliant fluorescence to the soft blue of a small desk lamp.

The next day I asked why, if the man next door could have the overhead light turned off at night, I couldn't. "We'll see," came the answer.

And they came through for me. By mid-afternoon Seroor appeared carrying a lamp. It was plugged in, and thereafter when I was ready to sleep, the overhead light was turned out and the illuminated lamp was draped with my blindfold, one side left open so the sisters could study. Less light certainly made things more comfortable for sleeping.

One of the decided joys of this room was being able to look outside and see the Elborz Mountains. I watched the peaks whiten with snow as the season deepened, and I marvelled at their silent, majestic stability. They reminded me of the psalmist's words I had sung with my church choir, "Who shall ascend into the hill of the Lord? / Or who shall stand in his holy place? / He that hath clean hands, and a pure heart; / who hath not lifted up his soul unto vanity" (Ps. 24:3,4). God had given me another splendid reminder of His abiding unchanging presence.

From here I could also see the embassy communications antenna. The shape of its brace formed a perfect cross atop an elongated globe. I mused on that lesson for hours. Communication, the cross, and an out-of-shape world. What helpful icons of grace for lonely meditation.

There eventually came the questioning that the girls had been so excited about. I was exercising when someone knocked at the door. The sister on duty answered, nodded, carefully closed the door, and then walked over to tell me I should get ready. The brothers were coming to talk to me.

I dried off the perspiration and pulled my sweater on over the red knit shirt. Then I sat down in my easy chair, spread a blanket over my knees, and waited. My heart began to race; I was expecting the worst. What could I possibly know that they wanted? Worse, what did they *think* I knew?

"Dear God, please keep me cool," I stammered under my breath. "I put myself in Your hands." It was the same prayer I had said so often before Christmas. I was completely in His care. There was not a thing I could do to change what was happening.

With a jolt, the door banged open and three brothers swaggered into the room. My first impression of them was their scruffiness and slovenliness, which I knew was not considered unusual here, but which I still found distasteful—dirty feet jammed into plastic flip-flops, unshaven faces, and unpressed clothes.

Don't look at those things, I warned myself.

One of the brothers was quite heavyset, a bit wall-eyed, and I soon dubbed him "Bully Boy." He appeared to be the leader. "You speak Farsi!" he announced in English.

"Some," I replied. "I was working on it at the Ahnjo-man."

"We'll do the interview in Farsi," he announced further. "Do you also read and write Farsi?"

"No," I said, "and I will not answer your questions in Farsi, either. The sisters have tried to trick me by using Farsi. My Farsi is not that good. There will be no questions answered in Farsi."

They sent off for an interpreter.

When he came, I recognized him as the same tall, slender man who had appeared in my room for interrogation during the first week of captivity. I knew his English was excellent. At first I had hoped he was from the Foreign Ministry, but I had found out later he probably was one of the student ring leaders.

They brought in a couple of chairs, sat down, and the questions began. Name, age, position, father's name, mother's name. One brother was writing furiously at the

98

typing table. And then: "What was your father's and mother's occupation?"

I was angry. "You leave my family out of this! I will answer questions about my job and my work, but I will not have you asking questions about my family."

"Hahnum Koob," said the interpreter, "we just need to know about the occupation."

"Daddy is a retired farmer; mother, a retired school teacher."

"What did they do before?" Bully Boy asked.

I must have begun to bristle visibly because the interpreter pleaded, "Miss Koob. . . ."

Despite the absurdity of the question, I complied, "I told you: He was a farmer; my mother, a teacher."

Bully Boy started to press me again, but he was cut off by the interpreter.

Then began a lengthy interchange of questions and answers concerning where I went to college, high school, and grade school. Wartburg College in Waverly, Iowa, the small high school in Jesup, the three-room country school in Jubilee near our farm. I answered all their questions with deliberate detail, drawing out long and boring answers to such demands as "Describe in detail what you studied." I gave them everything from dry, strung-out accounts of fourth-grade conservation classes —facts about soil erosion, water quality, and wildlife—to brief but clear and hopefully interesting summaries of my courses in philosophy and Christianity at college.

At the end of the day, I was instructed to write out my deposition in English. It was translated into Farsi, with each page brought back for my signature. I looked the Farsi over as best I could, but prayed if push came to shove there would be someone at hand as a witness who could verify my English.

After several days of this bantering back and forth we finally got to my career: foreign service. "What was your first post?"

"Ivory Coast. Abidjan is the capital."

99

"You had special classes before you went there?"

"Yes, African area studies and French language."

"What did you study in those classes?"

I described the area study classes. They consisted of a general historical overview of a region, with special readings in political, social, and economic studies of the area. I usually read sociology and cultural anthropology materials as well as art histories. I emphasized that as a new officer, I was the lowest ranking member of the embassy there and that I was working in a building apart from the main embassy— just as I had been when I was kidnapped here and brought to the embassy. I used the word "kidnapped" purposely, for I considered their actions nothing short of that.

I talked about our programs on the Ivory Coast: the library, our film schedule, cooperation with the university, the selection process for Fulbright professors, and our work with visiting lecturers and artists.

Then the big question came.

"Hahnum Koob," Bully Boy said, "you have special knowledge in the area of U.S.-African foreign policy. Write out for us the program of what is going on in the Ivory Coast now."

My mouth dropped open in amazement. I burst into laughter. "That's an impossible request," I said. "The program changes each year to meet the needs of the country. It is written by people who are working there. I couldn't possibly pretend to tell you what the requests of the Ivorian University would be now. I don't even know if we still have a library at our American Cultural Center. Some of our posts no longer have libraries. If you really want to know, I suggest you have your embassy in Washington call on the Ivory Coast desk officer at 1750 Pennsylvania Avenue. Your representative can walk in off the street. Our offices are open."

The questioning continued for several more days. We finished with my tour in Ouagadougou, the capital of Upper Volta, and they discovered I had spent time in Nairobi at the end of that posting.

100

"Why didn't you tell us?" they asked. "What are you trying to hide?"

"Nothing," I said. "Nairobi is considered part of the Ouagadougou assignment. Just as I was going to India for a week from here to meet with the Fulbright Commission, so in Africa I helped out for a month in Nairobi when the cultural attaché was ill."

"What did you do? In *detail*," he warned.

"I spoke with students, set up exchange travel for a couple of Kenyans to go to the United States, and worked in the library."

"What did you tell the students?" There was suspicion in every glance.

"Things like, 'Yes, it's cold in Michigan. Yes, Bowling Green is a good school. It is essential that you have the money you need for the first year before you go.' Typical student advisory things."

Then the final question. "How long and where did you go to school when you were next back in the States? What did you study?"

"I studied French for two months when I got back, and Romanian for six months before I left for Bucharest."

They looked at each other, lines of strong satisfaction crossing their faces. They thought they had me. I could read their minds. I had only accounted for eight months out of two and a half years. What was I hiding? They almost began to twitch with inner excitement. *Enough,* I thought.

"Excuse me, gentlemen," I said. "You asked me only about my schooling. Did you mean for me to tell you what else I did?"

"Please," came the surprised response.

"I was a desk officer in the African area. That is a liaison person in Washington between several African posts and our Washington offices."

I could see all kinds of problems coming up for me with that answer, and I thought we'd go on forever. But I was wrong. They never came back again for interrogations.

101

**Family gets a call
from Iowa hostage**
Des Moines Register
February 8, 1980

8

WINTER, 1980

Interrogations were not the only threat to my peace of mind. One night in January, after two months in captivity, took on an almost vaudevillian unreality. About 10:30 someone knocked at the door. I was already in bed. The sister went to answer and returned holding out to me a pair of glasses. Mine. I looked at them, stunned. Where had *these* come from?

"You asked for them," the sister said, handing them to me. She was the same young girl who had searched me so timorously that first day, and I had found her consistently to be a woman of few words.

"I didn't," I said. "I have my glasses. These are old ones for an emergency."

Then I began to be angry. "They were in my house in the back of my dresser drawer. I thought you were respecters of our personal property. What were you doing in my house? The Ayatollah said you weren't to go into any more buildings. You had no right to go into my house and rummage among my personal things!"

I had supposed that our houses were entered and searched long ago. But being confronted firsthand with the evidence of that search, and what I had come to regard as a

102

wanton destruction and complete disregard for anything that was not theirs, made my temper rise.

"Sister, I'm not angry with you," I continued heatedly. "I know you didn't do it. But this makes me fume. You say you respect private property and then do this. You break international law, seize diplomats and diplomatic property. Some revolution! About the same thing I would expect from people who think freedom means driving down a one way street the wrong way! How do you think you can rebuild a country when you have no respect for other people's property?"

I ranted on with her for several minutes. When I got it all out of my system I finally wound down. *I've probably made a mess of trouble for myself,* I thought. *I'd better apologize.*

"Sister," I said. "I'm sorry. I didn't mean to make you upset. I'm all right now." And I was. She had remained passive during the entire outburst—how many times had the girls asked me to talk quietly and "be ladylike"?—so I assumed she was all right about it, too. I pounded my pillow into shape and settled down again for the night.

It was then that the fun began. She drifted out of the room, as the girls were wont to do, and returned shortly. Then one of the brothers came in. I had not seen him before, but he obviously hated me. I wrapped myself in my blanket and stood to face him.

"Hahnum," he said sternly. "You must not act like this. You are making the sister most uncomfortable."

"You make me uncomfortable," I shot back. "I am a diplomat. You kidnapped me, brought me here, and now you break into my house."

"You aren't a diplomat and you know it."

"I *am* a diplomat and you know it. I've been accredited by several countries including Iran, and you've broken all sorts of your own laws with this action. Now you just broke another one, breaking into diplomatic property."

"You asked for your glasses," he said. "Besides, in some instances laws don't matter: special cases." He snarled at me, the venom of hatred shooting from his eyes.

"Special cases if the laws don't suit *you*," I answered vehemently.

"We represent the people," he alibied. "Besides, you sent for your glasses."

"I most certainly did not. I have mine right here. These are old ones I keep for emergencies. You needed an excuse to break into my house and you used these," I said, shaking the glasses in his direction.

"The sister said you wanted them." He spat the words out.

"Which sister?" I countered. "Bring her here!"

"I've told you, you asked for them," he said.

"I didn't. If I wanted something from my house, it wouldn't be these. It would be a pair of shoes and a change of clothes. And books!"

I knew arguing was useless, but it felt good! As I realized I was getting nowhere, the clincher came: "I've told you *three times* that you asked for them. Therefore, you asked for them!" he flared.

No arguing with logic like that, I thought.

"Don't make the sisters unhappy," he continued condescendingly. "You're nothing but a spy!"

I spoke firmly, quietly. "I am a diplomat, no matter what you say. And I did not ask for these glasses. I swear to God I didn't."

"Which God?" he snapped.

I looked him right in the eye. "There is only one God." He returned my stare and left the room.

"Dear Lord," I prayed, "help me stay in control."

There were some bright spots in that long, dreary month of January, however. For one thing, I was permitted to receive a little mail, so I had better clues to what was going on in the outside world. One letter came from a Mrs. Daisy Lykes-Martin who told about church bells being rung for us and people wearing armbands with black *50*s on them. It was the first clue I had as to how many of us were being held in Iran. Then someone wrote about a *Newsweek* story, and for the first time I was aware that the entire nation knew about us.

Letters also arrived from several of the nuns at St. Anthony's convent in Syracuse, New York, who were working for the cause of Mother Marianne of Molokai. Mother Marianne had gone to Hawaii in the late 1800s to work with Father Damien in the leper colony at Molokai, the first nun to answer the call there. She spent the rest of her life on the island, and she is buried there. Her motherhouse, St. Anthony's, is working to have her canonized. The sisters there found a special bond in writing to me, for Mother Marianne's family name before coming to the United States had been Koob!

Unusual friendships and bonds crossing traditional lines were being formed. I thought with gratitude of the prayers of the sisters from Syracuse, the prayer the Catholic bishop from Detroit who gave me Communion had prayed, and the greetings and words of prayer the cardinal from Algiers had brought from the Islamic leaders there. Knowing our well-being was the concern of such diverse groups renewed my hope for the world's future.

My own prayer time was becoming increasingly important, and my daily prayer list grew to include people who were writing us, the Iranian students, and of course, the leaders of our two countries. How does one pray for the Ayatollah and the people who were holding us hostage? That was a daily struggle.

Intercessions asking God's protection and care for my family came easily. Committing myself daily to Christ and asking for courage and strength to bear up, easy. Accepting what had happened, not so easy. Praying for my enemies? Hard! I just didn't know how to begin. The words of Christ were coming through to me loud and clear. He said, "Love your enemies" (Luke 6:27). So I knew I had to begin with prayer. I asked that God's grace be made known to the Ayatollah and that God would grant the needs of our captors. I prayed for the people of Iran. And then I prayed again that

105

the whole situation would be resolved. How I wanted to go home!

Dealing with my enemies was not necessarily easier after prayer, however. The students who were taking care of me were a strange mixture of very young, exuberant militants who spoke almost no English and sharp, sophisticated, middle-class young ladies who had family ties in the United States. They were also a strange combination of arrogant, sensitive, and well-mannered curious young women.

One night I was awakened by the sound of one of these sophisticated young ladies walking close to my bed. I usually slept very lightly, and in captivity the slightest change in the noise level seemed to wake me instantly. I waited breathlessly to see what she would do. Then I heard the unmistakable rustle of paper. She was taking one of the caramels I had been hoarding since Christmas!

I knew I'd been a fool for not hiding it, but usually the girls didn't touch my food. At Christmas, Queenie would hardly take a goodie from me even when I had insisted on it. I lay there silently and listened to her chew that caramel, resenting every delicious swallow. She finished up and left my area of the room.

Two days went by. I didn't see her about the place. Then she showed up for guard duty, and after routine mutual greetings she finally came over to me. "Hahnum Koob," she said meekly, "I took one of your candies the other night. I'm sorry. But I was so hungry! I know I shouldn't have."

"That's OK," I assured her, by now over my anger. "Anything that's left out is to be shared."

Goodies came less often after Christmas, but for some reason there seemed to be a limitless supply of gum. I didn't chew gum, but all the girls were crazy about it, so that it was shared on a half stick basis. One sister would take half a stick, leaving the other half for the next guard.

Somehow my room had again become the center for slumber parties. After demonstrations and standing out in the cold yelling their lungs out, the girls would tumble into my room to warm their hands and ask if I had any gum to "help their throats." There were times I felt like a matronly dorm mother, a mother hen looking after frenzied chicks.

A few of the girls would politely take their shoes off the minute they came into the room; others scattered dirt and mud all across the rug. They loved to come in around 2:30 in the morning and settle down on the floor for giggles and girl talk.

One morning I woke to find the carpet absolutely covered with dried mud, after I finally had secured a vacuum cleaner the day before and had everything spotless. I came awfully close to tears. One of the girls I had been tutoring in English, Zahro, was on duty. She was only nineteen, but she was a second-year premed student and quite responsible.

"What's wrong, Hahnum?" she asked.

"Look at this filth!" I said. "Do you girls live like this at home? I don't think I should have to put up with this nonsense." And I set about to pick up pieces of hardened mud and dead grass strewn across the floor.

Then I turned to her. "Don't say anything, Zahro. I'm just tired. I didn't sleep well."

"Are you sick?" she asked quickly. "Do you want a doctor?"

"No. I'm just not as young as I used to be, and I'm no longer accustomed to dorm life. When the girls come in at 2:30 and talk till 4:00 I just don't sleep. I'm getting old."

I smiled ruefully at her and continued. "I remember well talking until the wee hours when I was your age."

She helped me clean up the mess, found the vacuum cleaner again, and I swept the place once more. Later that day one of the other girls came in. "We have our own room now," she announced. "We won't bother you anymore at night. That wasn't right. And I'm sorry about the muddy rugs. We just didn't think."

I counted my blessings one more time. The girls actually *were* quiet after that, and occasionally they would come in for "peace and quiet" naps on my turf. But there were no more 2:30 A.M. hen parties. I was amused at such a variety of responses from these girls who were prepared to die for what they were doing, yet could be bothered in conscience for snitching a caramel or for keeping a crabby old hostage awake at night.

And what did I get for my efforts? In early February I was moved yet once more, this time to a corner office on the first floor level. There were slogans and posters all over the walls, but there were advantages: handsome green curtains at the windows, a desk I could use, a leather desk chair, a lamp, and the windows all intact. The room was spacious, and the students moved me there with great pride. "I'll bet this is better than any prison!" Hamid, the brother who had accused me of signaling to Bill with my eyes, exclaimed.

I did toy with the thought that in an American prison I could (a) see my lawyer, (b) know the charges leveled against me, (c) see my family now and then, (d) do some constructive work, (e) have the use of a library, (f) hear the evening news, and (g) send and receive mail!

Nonetheless, I settled into the new room and found it to be rather pleasant. I could occasionally hear Ann Swift's voice down the hall and the footsteps of some of the American men passing to and fro.

The nights continued to be unpredictable. I was sound asleep one evening when the overhead light flashed on. "What is it?" I asked. Queenie was standing inside the door.

"Get dressed, Hahnum Koob," she said. "Quickly. One of the brothers is coming."

I pulled on my slacks and sweater. I was ready. Two of the brothers came into the room. "It's the Prophet's birthday," one said. "On this occasion you may make a call to your parents."

My face must have fallen to the floor, for one of them asked, "What is it?"

"I don't have their telephone number. It's in my purse. You have it."

"What do you mean, you don't know your parents' phone number?" the brother asked sharply.

"In the wintertime they stay in Florida with my sister. I don't know her number," I said.

Queenie and the guards spoke quickly in Farsi. She was explaining where my purse was. They looked at me suspiciously, and one of the brothers left the room.

He came back with my little red pocket directory. I showed them the number, then I was blindfolded and taken downstairs to the switchboard. The walls of that room were decorated with anti-Carter and anti-American posters and slogans too, as well as the inevitable pictures honoring Khomeini.

"You may make only one phone call and no more. You may not talk about politics, and you must not say anything about our security system here at the embassy. We also want you to read this clipping."

He handed me an article from the English language *Teheran Times* which stated that the terms for our release were unconditional. "You have three minutes."

The switchboard controller dialed the number, and I heard my brother-in-law David answer, "Voigts' residence." The telephone operator said something, and the connection was broken. (David thought it was a hoax and hung up.) I must have looken stricken because they dialed again. This time when David answered, I spoke quickly. "David, it's Kate! Don't hang up!"

There was silence for a split second, and then I heard David say, "How are you?" While I answered, he began speaking to his son Mark. "Mark, run get Mommy. It's Katie."

"I'm fine," I said. "Are Mother and Daddy there?"

"No," he said, "they are in Washington at a meeting."

My mind absorbed the shock. I was so tense my legs were trembling. I had an incredible grip on the receiver, and all of a sudden I realized it would have been almost impossible for me emotionally to talk with Mother and Daddy.

I explained why I was allowed to call, and we talked about the family. Anabeth was on one extension, David on the other. They assured me that the folks were OK and that we were constantly remembered in people's prayers. I asked

109

them the date of Ash Wednesday, and I even got to say hello to Mark and Emma Lou. I read the clipping finally and discovered Anabeth had sent me a sweater. I never received it.

The conversation was taped, and a few days later the tape was brought to me and I was requested to make a transcription of it. The brothers assured me I would receive a photocopy of what I had written, but I never did.

The conversation with Anabeth and David made me hunger all the more for Christian fellowship. I began to pray daily for the services of a minister or priest; I was specifically asking the Lord for the sacrament of Holy Communion. Taking Communion at Christmas with Bishop Gumbleton had filled me then with the love of God, and I again longed for the comfort and strength that the physical act of participating in the Lord's Supper could provide.

I thought back to those days in eighth grade confirmation class when we were learning Psalm 42. "As the hart panteth after the water brooks, so panteth my soul after thee, O God. My soul thirsteth for God, for the living God: when shall I come and appear before God?" Pastor Planz had so patiently explained those verses to us: a hart was a deer and "panting" was a longing. Now I understood clearly what the psalmist was saying. For the first time in my life I truly *longed* for an opportunity to worship and receive Holy Communion.

It wasn't but a few days later that Zahro arrived at noon to tell me, with a great deal of pleasure, that a priest was coming! She knew how much this meant to me, so she found a broom and hurriedly helped me clean the room.

Then we waited. A steady stream of girls filed into the room all day, chattering excitedly about the archbishop who was coming. He was the exiled Palestinian Hilarion Capudji. "He was exiled for a cause, and he understands what we are doing!" the sisters insisted in fervent admiration. In all the uproar I was wondering if I had been forgotten.

It must have been well after six o'clock when I heard a group of people coming down the hall. They went into Ann's room first, and then finally one of the brothers announced, "They are coming!" The door burst open and in poured a huge group of students with video-tape cameras, camera lights, microphones, and tape recorders, followed by the Archbishop Capudji and another Catholic priest. I looked eagerly from man to man, searching for the small black case that a minister usually carries when he visits the sick or imprisoned. Their hands were empty. I wanted to cry. I couldn't believe that these men had come without Communion.

We were introduced: Archbishop Capudji first. Then the other priest reached out his hand and said, "I'm Monsignor Nolan, and I bring you greetings from . . . ," and he proceeded to list about a half dozen cardinals.* I listened for a few minutes and finally broke into the recital of names. "And I hope from Bishop David Preus from the American Lutheran Church in Minneapolis." He looked at me, rather surprised, and said "Yes, from him, too."

The two men then asked me the usual questions: How was I? Was everything all right? Terribly aware of the TV cameras and the microphones, I raised my voice. I wanted there to be no question in the minds of family and friends: Yes, it was Kate talking! Soon my words were tumbling over themselves, and we were all talking at once. How firm and good these men's clasps were.

But again I looked. No sign of Communion. How could they come without the sacrament?

When Archbishop Capudji asked if he could do something for me, I asked if he could see about getting us a priest for worship. He seemed to exude an air of authority with the students.

"You do not have regular visits from a priest?" he asked.

"No. I have not seen anyone since Christmas. You are an answer to a prayer." I choked on my words and almost broke. *Not in front of the students*, I reminded myself. Or for the folks at home, for that matter. I gave myself a mental charge to

---

*Monsignor John G. Nolan, papal secretary to the Holy Land.

control my feelings. Archbishop Capudji promised to try to arrange for a priest to visit.

All too soon they were gone. Had I heard him right? Did Monsignor Nolan really say the greatest part of this was behind us? *Dear God, You wouldn't have let him say it if it wasn't so, would You?"*

Perhaps something positive was happening here. Maybe we would soon be going home. Someone had been here. I had touched people from the outside world.

Events began to run together. A doctor came and took my blood pressure. Period. That was the physical for all of us, I surmised. Members of the revolutionary council visited one Sunday shortly thereafter, and I was told by one man that our release was in the hands of the United States government. He also said the council was convinced I was who I said I was and not in Iran for any other purpose. I'm not even sure I responded to his statement.

I began to count my greatest joy as being left alone for a short time, sometimes as long as twenty minutes at a stretch. During one of these private times, the sister on duty left her textbook sitting open on her desk with a bookmark in place. I tiptoed over to look at it. The marker looked suspiciously as if it was written in English.

It was!

The paper was actually a flyer from a black power organization, using the November, 1979, release of the eight blacks and five women American hostages as the rallying point for raising funds. *Release!* The feeling of euphoria was almost as great as if I'd been sent home myself. It had happened. My hunch had been right. Thank God! Some were home. *The world does know what is going on!* We hadn't been relegated to the back pages of the newspapers. *Thank You, Lord, Oh, thank You!* I hugged this secret knowledge to myself, and it obliterated anything else that happened for several days to come.

Hamid came in to tell me there was a commission in Tehran studying the crimes of the Shah. Would I write a letter about the crimes? I told him I had arrived after the

Five sisters in a huddle: big sister Kate in the back, Micki on the left, Vivian on the right, Anabeth looking down, and Mary Jane covering her eyes. Emi wasn't around for this one. The place—President Harry Truman's house in Independence, Missouri, in 1949.

The family farm in Iowa. Sister Emi and her husband, Dale, now own it and live there with their three daughters—the sixth generation of our family on the same farm.

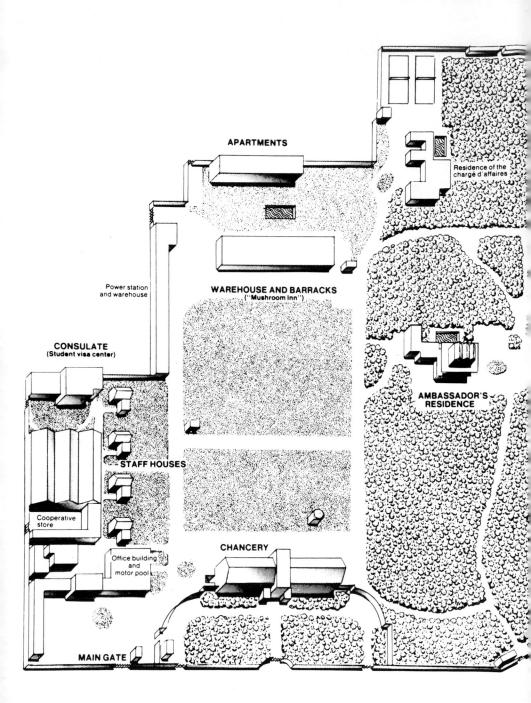

APARTMENTS

Residence of the
chargé d'affaires

Power station
and warehouse

WAREHOUSE AND BARRACKS
("Mushroom Inn")

CONSULATE
(Student visa center)

AMBASSADOR'S
RESIDENCE

STAFF HOUSES

Cooperative
store

CHANCERY

Office building
and
motor pool

MAIN GATE

U. S. Embassy compound in Tehran (above). Location of U. S. Embassy (top right) in relation to the Iran-American Society and the Foreign Ministry where Bruce Laingen, Victor Tomseth, and Michael Howland were held captive. (© 1981 by The New York Times Company. Reprinted by permission.)

Kathy Gross, 22, was one of the embassy secretaries released on November 18, 1979. On the day of the take-over she was paraded outside the embassy by her guard, seen in the traditional chador. (United Press International photo)

An Iranian Air Force serviceman joined
thousands of his countrymen outside the
embassy shouting the anti-American slogans
that rang in our ears for weeks after the
take-over. (United Press International photo)

Some of my colleagues participate in the Christmas service two and a half months after the take-over. In foreground, Detroit Bishop Thomas Gumbleton (L) and Archbishop of Algiers Etienne Duval preside. The anti-American rhetoric and pictures of Khomeini covered the walls throughout the embassy. (United Press International photo)

Christmas decorations were made from old envelopes (notice address inside angel on the left), plain white paper, old Christmas cards, snatches of foil and string, and cotton from vitamin bottles. (Photo by Marilyn K. Yee)

Ann Swift and I became roommates after four months of confinement. She made this mobile as my Christmas present in 1980. The left side symbolized home: trees with yellow ribbons, letters, and our flag. The right symbolized our predicament: the bars, the black chadors of our guards. The cross represented our constant companion: Christ and His Spirit. (Photo by Marilyn K. Yee)

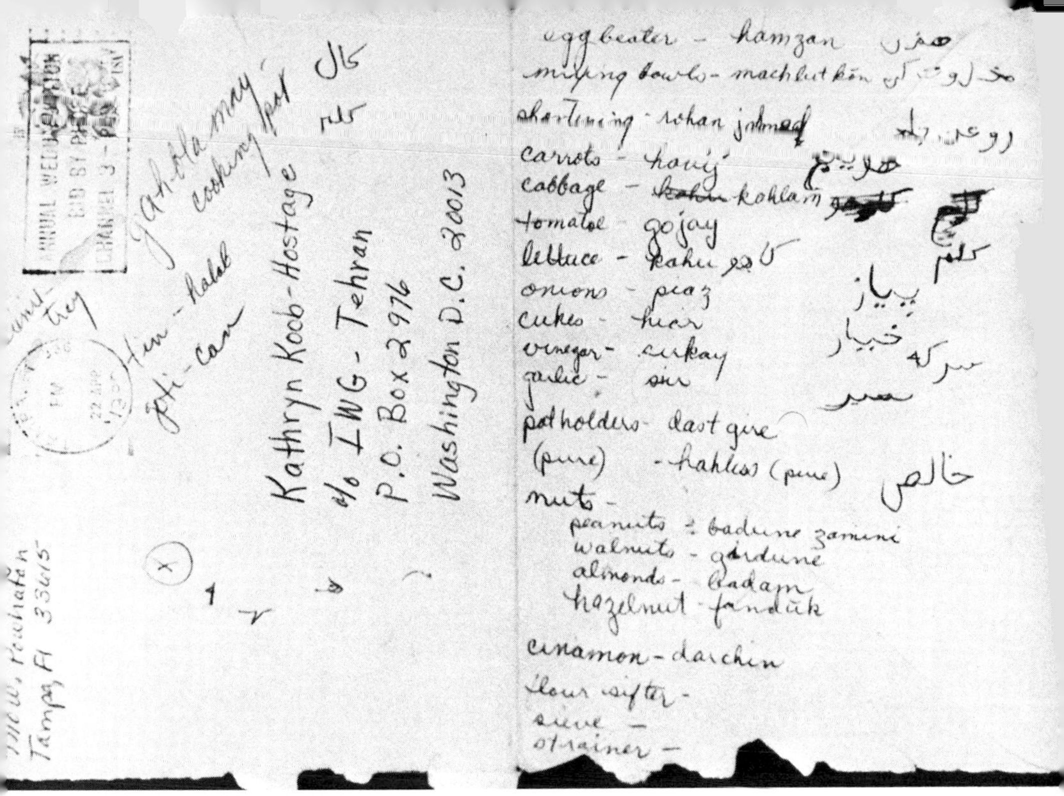

Handwritten list on envelope:

egg beater - hamzan همزن

mixing bowls - machlut ken مخلوط کن

shortening - rohan johmad روغن جامد

carrots - houij هویج

cabbage - kohlam کلم

tomato - gojay گوجه

lettuce - kahu کاهو

onions - peaz پیاز

cukes - hiar خیار

vinegar - serkay سرکه

garlic - sir سیر

potholders - dast gire

(pure) - hahless (pure) خالص

nuts -
  peanuts - badems zamini
  walnuts - gardune
  almonds - badam
  hazelnut - fanduk

cinamon - darchin

flour sifter -

sieve -

strainer -

Envelope addressing:

Yah Alamay
cooking pot بلا

Hen - Halal
Ji - Can

Kathryn Koob - Hostage
c/o IWG - Tehran
P.O. Box 2976
Washington D.C. 20013

1M1 E.W. Fernleaf
Tampa, FL 33615

Ann and I began our cooking duties in June. Menus were planned on old envelopes, first in English, then in Farsi. We asked the guards to supply our kitchen needs. (Photo by Marilyn K. Yee)

A "page" from my diary. (Photo by Marilyn K. Yee)

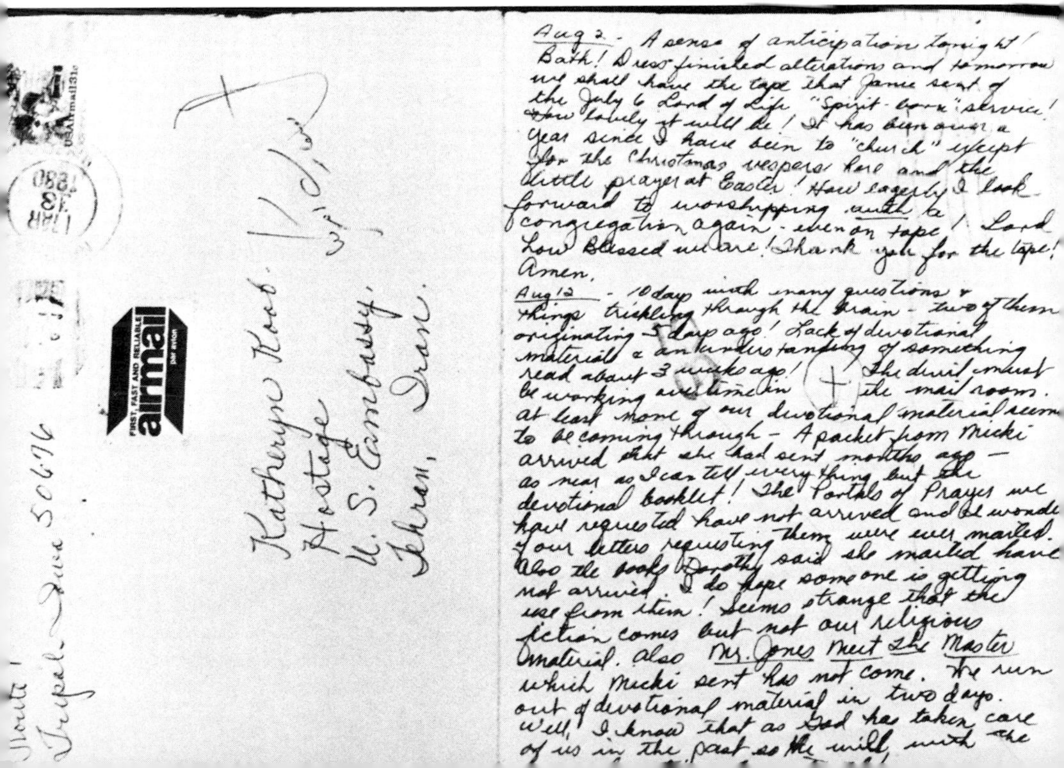

Envelope:

airmail
FIRST FAST AND RELIABLE

Kathryn Koob
Hostage
U.S. Embassy.
Tehran, Iran.

Diary page:

Aug 2 - A sense of anticipation tonight! Bath! Dress finished alterations and tomorrow we shall have the tape that Jamie sent of the July 6 Lord of Life "Spirit-born" service! How lovely it will be! It has been over a year since I have been to "church" except for the Christmas vespers here and the little prayer at Easter! How eagerly I look forward to worshipping with a congregation again - even on tape! Lord, how blessed we are! Thank you for the tape! Amen.

Aug 3 - 10 days with many questions & things trickling through the brain - two of them originating 5 days ago! Lack of devotional materials & an unkind tampering of something read about 3 weeks ago! The devil must be working overtime in the mail room. At least some of our devotional material seems to be coming through - A packet from Micki arrived that she had sent months ago - as near as I can tell every thing but the devotional booklet! The Portals of Prayer we have requested have not arrived and I wonder if our letters requesting them were even mailed. Also the books which she said she mailed have not arrived. I do hope some one is getting use from them! Seems strange that the fiction comes but not our religious material. Also Mr. Jones Meet the Master which Micki sent has not come. We run out of devotional material in two days. Well, I know that as God has taken care of us in the past so He will with the

Katherine Koob   Pownal Elem. School
Rec'd 7/17
                           Grade 4 H
                           Pownal, Vt. 05261
                           May 21, 1980

Dear Katherine,

How are you? My name is Jennifer Wilcox. I'm ten and in the fourth grade and I'm writing this letter to cheer you up.

I'm sorry that the rescue didn't succeed. But I hope they try again.

I have no pets so I will talk about you. Do you have any children? What do you look like? Do you have any hobbies? What are they?

My hobby is roller-skating.

Please write back. I'll be waiting for your letter back.

Your friend,
Jennifer Wilcox

This letter informing us of the rescue attempt slipped by the censors. Otherwise, it is typical of many we received from school children. (Photo by Marilyn K. Yee)

WELCO
BACK
FREE

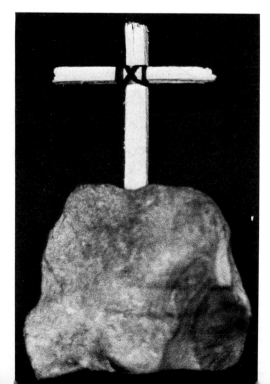

Ann made this cross for me as an Easter gift. It became the center of our worship area throughout the rest of our captivity. (Photo by Marilyn K. Yee)

Bible in hand (notice strings holding it together), I greeted the crowd at Rhein-Main Air Base in West Germany. With me were my boss, John Graves (bottom), and Duane Gillette, a Navy communications and intelligence specialist. (United Press International photo)

What a pleasure to talk with Harry Barnes while enroute to the hospital in Weisbaden. He was the ambassador to Romania during my assignment there from 1974–75. (Photo by Donna Gigliotti)

Being greeted by President Jimmy Carter at the hospital in Wiesbaden was special. Having missed the election, I still thought of him as my president. Vice-President Walter Mondale looks on at right. (Courtesy of the Carter White House Photo Office Collection, Carter Presidential Materials Project)

Thousands waved and cheered along our route from Stewart Airport to West Point Military Academy. (United Press International photo)

Eight flags at half-mast were sober reminders to us of the eight men killed during the aborted rescue attempt. (United Press International photo)

Ann Swift and I are seen here leaving West Point for a news conference. Ann's mother is behind me. (Photo by Donna Gigliotti)

Mother, Daddy, and me at the Thayer Hotel at West Point. How good to give them a hug and to be able to talk to them again! (Photo by Donna Gigliotti)

In the Blue Room in the White House, President and Mrs. Reagan greeted each of us with warm hugs and handshakes. (Photo by Bill Fitz-patrick, The White House)

The New York City ticker-tape parade.
I'm riding with City Comptroller Harrison
Goldin. (United Press International
photo)

When I arrived at the Iowa Statehouse,
I was greeted by this enormous
billboard. I was overwhelmed. Another
sign greeted me in my hometown: the
electronic signboard in front of the bank
flashed "Welcome home Katie . . .
Katie gave Earl a kiss." Mr. Earl
Stewart, senior vice-president of the
bank, helped me open my first savings
account when I was a child and has
taken care of my banking needs ever
since. He greeted me at the airport
when I arrived, and he did get a kiss!
(Courtesy of the Governor's Office,
State of Iowa)

The homecoming celebration in Jesup, Iowa. Seen behind me is a childhood friend, confirmation and high school classmate, Eleanor Harting Fialzke. She and Roger Fisher (hidden behind me) planned the event. (Photo by Brenda Riensche, courtesy of *Citizen Herald,* © 1981)

Here I am greeting the people gathered in the rotunda of the State Capitol. Governor Robert D. Ray is beside me, and my parents can be seen under my upraised arm. (Courtesy of the Governor's Office, State of Iowa)

Back on the job at the Foreign Press Center in New York City. (Photo by Marilyn K. Yee)

revolution. But I did write a letter acknowledging the establishment of the commission and stating that I had no first-hand knowledge to contribute.

The Ayatollah's son came to visit. Cameras were everywhere, but he made it clear he wanted no pictures. He sat across the room from me and carefully asked how I was and if I had been mistreated.

I answered as I always did: "The students take very good care of my physical needs. I am provided with plenty of food, and I am warm."

I had a strong urge to run across the room and flop down in this little man's lap and pat him on the cheeks. He had a very full beard, which only emphasized his round, childish face, and his eyes moved quickly about the room, darting here and there. I restrained my impulse because I knew it would only cause problems, but there were times when I dearly longed to fly in the face of all Islamic conventions.

After the visit of the doctor and the Ayatollah's son, I began to hope anew that our release was not far off. The students seemed to be more relaxed, and I heard snatches of news concerning Iranian elections. Surely things would come to a head soon.

I began to have a strong hunch that we might be headed home the last week in February. Communion at home on the first Sunday in March! What a joy that would be. My longing for it had not abated one whit!

But as the month passed and nothing happened, I prayed that even if we couldn't go home that somehow the bread and wine would find its way to us. Archbishop Capudji had promised a priest, and the time was about right for another visit—the end of December, the first of February, and now, the first of March.

I prayed so hard for the visit of a priest.* I focused in my devotions on Jesus the Rock, searching the Psalms for refer-

---

*From the first day, I had had to battle the idea that if I could say the right words, pray the perfect prayer, God would hear me and this ordeal would be over. Here I was doing it again!

ences, anchoring myself to His strength and constancy, aching for the link with Him that Communion would bring. I concentrated on memorizing a favorite hymn:

> *Beneath the cross of Jesus*
> *I fain would take my stand*
> *The shadows of a mighty rock*
> *Within a weary land.*

I had read Somerset Maugham's *Of Human Bondage* a month before, and so I prayed confidently, like the hero of that book, secure in the promise that faith would move mountains. The mountain was the chain on the door keeping the priest and Communion out.

February passed, and we weren't released. Still I prayed, pouring out all my longing to Christ.

On Sunday, March 3, I woke and knew the priest wasn't going to come. No minister was going to be permitted to bring me Communion, and my mountain wasn't going to be moved, at least in the way that I thought it should be.

I got up and went through my normal routine. My blindfold was tied in place, and I went down to the bathroom. I took a sponge bath, brushed my teeth and combed my hair. I looked at myself in the mirror and promised myself that it was going to be all right. I went back to the room and the hot tea and bread and cheese that was my usual breakfast was waiting for me. I said my table prayer and ate, putting a little bit of cheese and bread aside because somehow teatime always found me hungry. And I picked up my Bible and hymnbook, put the blanket over my knees, curled up in the big chair in front of the desk, and started my morning worship.

I don't remember what hymns I used that morning. I don't remember what Scripture passage I read. But I poured out my soul in prayer, asking God to give me strength to meet the day without Communion. I asked Him if it was wrong to want the sacrament so much and asked Him to provide for me.

114

As I prayed, I was filled with the sense of His presence. I knew as He reached out to me on that day that it was going to be a long time until I would receive the bread and wine of Holy Communion again. But in the end, it wasn't necessary. There was a deeper communion of being one with Him, and that was what I needed. It was sufficient for me to rest in His love.

The warmth and the glow of His love stayed with me through that long winter's day. I knew now that even as God had reached out to hold me and to provide for me in that critical hour, so would He reach out and provide for me from His strength and His love whenever I needed it.

In a way it would have been appropriate if that Sunday had been the traditional date of Christ's Transfiguration. It wasn't, but it certainly was a significant part of my awakening in Iran.

Shah leaves for Egypt/
Shuns U.S. appeal to
remain in Panama
Des Moines Register
March 24, 1980

9

EASTER, 1980

Spring was coming. Valentine's Day had passed. I had cut up one of my prettiest cards with flowers, taped my last two caramels on it, and sent it to Ann. I had written simply "To Ann, Happy Valentine's Day. Love, Kate." Back had come two red plastic carnations and a similar card.

When the brother brought my lunch that day, he also brought me a small bouquet of fresh flowers. The scent of the white narcissus filled the room. I was amazed: a living, fresh flower in my cheerless room. A touch of outside. "Thank you, thank you!" I said in wonder. "Where did these come from?"

"From Americans who hate Carter as much as we do!" The reply was snapped out and sparks of hatred flew from his eyes. Hatred, always hatred! How ugly. But even hatred couldn't change the fragile beauty of those tiny, fragrant flowers.

Next on the docket would be St. Patrick's Day, the first day of spring, and then Easter. Would we really be here that long?

The Lord was constant in His faithfulness. He was teaching me. I had promised myself I would not bargain with Him. I was all set to learn and to practice what I would learn, but I was not going to make any kind of spiritual deals in

116

exchange for freedom. He had said He'd take care of me, and He had.

One day, in passing, the guard told me some of the other Americans were quite blue and discouraged. I could understand that, for I often was. *But you have an antidote*, I reminded myself. Whenever I started to feel sorry for myself, I went through my evening prayer list with renewed energy: the lonely, the hungry, the politically oppressed, the sick and handicapped, and then I prayed for world understanding. On one of my blue days I read John 15. The words of verse 16 seemed to be printed in boldface type: "I have chosen you . . . that ye should go and bring forth fruit . . . that whatsoever ye shall ask of the Father in my name, he may give it you."

"Lord, I know what I'm thinking is presumptuous," I prayed. "Reading that verse this morning makes it almost seem we can order You to do *our* will in Jesus' name. But Father, I know that Jesus sought Your will! At any rate, that verse is filled with power, Lord. Can You please let us all know in some small way today that we haven't been forgotten in Iran? And do find some way to let all of us draw strength from You. Thank You, Lord. Amen."

I was amazed at the power that verse promises us as Christians, and yet I had to laugh with delight when, three hours later, we had perked coffee for lunch for the first time. The Lord appreciated small pleasures, too!

I had hoped and prayed that our release would come long before Ash Wednesday, but I wanted to be prepared if I had to stay. This year's Lenten season was to become a special time to focus my meditations on the love that God the Father has for us. As I continued to wrestle in prayer and in day-to-day living with the problem of loving my enemies, I realized all the more clearly the overwhelming love the Father has for me.

When Ash Wednesday came, I saw an opportunity to send a message to Ann. I didn't know how strong her Christian convictions were, but I had heard her tell the Algerian cardinal at Christmas that she was Episcopalian. She might

117

not know this was Ash Wednesday, particularly since the students had refused to take Bishop Gumbleton's lectionary from room to room for us. I wondered if she had even seen the calendar in the front of the book, much less noted the dates.

"Sister, do you think you could give Miss Swift this message?" I asked. "Today is a holy day for us. Please tell her that today is Ash Wednesday."

"Certainly. Will you write it for me?"

"Of course. Here it is." And I printed out a note. "Ann, today, February 20, is Ash Wednesday."

The sister disappeared with the note, and a short time later she was back. "Miss Swift says thank you," she reported.

I refused breakfast that morning, for I had determined to commit the day to prayer and fasting. When lunch came, I also turned it down. The girls were curious. And I thought they were a bit worried, too, for they asked about my not eating.

"It's a *ruzae* for me," I explained, using their word for "fasting." "Today is the beginning of a period of preparation for Easter. I will eat nothing until tomorrow morning. However, I will take water."

"Why do you do that?"

"Drink water?"

"No, fast."

"It helps me remember that this is the special time when Jesus Christ suffered and died for sin and rose again that we might share His life. I must prepare myself with prayer during this time for the festival of Easter, which is as important to Christians as Christmas."

I then went on to talk about the various acts of sacrifice that people make during Lent to enter into the Lord's suffering in some small way. I told how some people give up some special food to remind them of the principle of sacrifice, in some instances giving the cash value of the food to the needy.

All this evoked a strong response on the special value of

118

Islam and its regular care for the poor. The girls explained to me how Islam would be the saving religion of the world because it alone looked after the poor.

This gave me a chance to talk about the work of the church of Jesus Christ, its services and its care for people. A mental, invisible Christianity, void of works, will never cut it with the outside world. I wasn't sure I had convinced anybody of anything, but all day as the guards changed, the word was whispered with quick glances my way, "She's fasting. It's *ruzae* for her." I realized again how important the fruits of faith and good works are, and how they witness to the world the truth of the commandment to love our neighbors as ourselves.

I continued to work on my prayer list, modifying my evening devotional hymns and readings to help me think in terms of Lent and Easter. I was particularly trying to open my prayer structure and intentions to new or different ways of approaching problems. I wanted God to instruct me, and I prayed that others would also open their hearts to new understandings of world problems of hunger, economics, and international tensions. I also prayed there would be new understanding between nations, and I echoed the prayer, written on a card from my friend Helen Englert, for ". . . a creative solution to the impasse." The knowledge that Christians around the world were praying for us, and that individuals like Helen were ringing church bells to remind others of our plight, was very important.

On the morning of March 12 I awoke as usual at about ten, pulled on my now baggy slacks and sweater, and trudged off blindfolded to the bathroom. As I was walking back to the room I heard a familar voice. "Hahnum Koob," Miryam said over the usual hubbub in the hall, "Hahnum Swift is coming."

"For how long?" I asked, hoping for at least a couple of hours.

The soft answer that came was yet another variant of Iranian polite refusal: "*Maloom Niste*—It isn't clear."

119

There were many things, of course, that weren't clear. But today something special clearly was happening. The door was flung open, and my heart stopped. Two of the brothers came into the room carrying a mattress, and for a split second I thought Ann was bundled up in the center of it, immobile. *Lord, what has happened to her?* I thought to myself. Then I realized it was not Ann, but a roll of blankets and clothing inside. Following almost immediately in the procession was a blindfolded Ann Swift.

"Come this way. Here you are," they told her. She looked so terribly thin and frail. Her blindfold came off, and there we were.

We had known each other only casually, having met in language school, but I was thrilled to see her. I knew better than to betray my feelings to the guards, but impulsively I hugged her and then drew back. The guards who had brought us together were beaming with the success of their surprise.

Ann blinked, trying to control her smile, and we stood there for a few minutes just looking at each other. We hardly knew what to do next. The guards were listening carefully, hoping we'd say something they could pounce on, so Ann started discussing living arrangements. Did I mind if we swapped heaters? The one I had was an electric radiator. Ann's was the kind that had a wire screen around clay pipes which were ringed with heating coils. "It makes such good toast," she said. And it did! When breakfast arrived shortly, a couple of minutes on the wire screen toasted the bread perfectly.

Our next project was clean-up. "Let's wash the walls!" Ann suggested. We scrubbed through at least one layer of paint and removed all the penciled slogans that I hated so much but had not had the nerve to erase by myself.

We got along well. We had our own drawers of personal effects and our own "living space," and during the first few days we kept our own schedules as well. She liked to exercise before lunch and would leave her large midday meal until

120

she had done her first daily dozen. After several weeks we began to do our exercise program together daily, with Sundays off. We worked in concert on stretches, toe touches, arm circles, deep knee bends and then on to our own leg lifts, side leg lifts, sit-ups and push-ups. Ann also liked to do jumping jacks. Then we ran in place.

In one letter home I had asked David, Anabeth's husband, to send me information about running. When it arrived, Ann and I read it carefully and began a regimented running program. But we needed a watch to time ourselves. "Sister, do you suppose I could have my watch back?" I asked one afternoon. It was the first time I had had the courage to ask for my jewelry. It had been taken one night in early November.

"I don't see why not. I'll ask the brother."

We did get a watch: someone else's! It was a Rolex with a sweep second hand so we could time our running. It was also very nice to know what time of day it was, when to get up, and what time to retire.

About three days in our new living arrangement, I woke up and said to Ann, "I'm so glad you are here. I thought I was sleeping OK before, but I really feel rested this morning." For the first time I realized how tense and anxious I had been for the past four and a half months. How reassuring it was to have another person in this with me!

Off and on during the day we were able to share information with each other. Bruce and Vic were still at the Foreign Ministry. David Newsome was in charge of the task force. I could tell Ann about the church bells ringing and the armbands with the 50s on them, and she had a photograph of trees with yellow ribbons around them lining the road leading to her friends' house. "Tie a Yellow Ribbon 'Round the Old Oak Tree" evidently had become a theme song during this crisis back home.

I was able to tell Ann that the other women had gone home, and she told me a little bit more about the questioing they had gone through—some of it terrifying. We pooled our

121

knowledge of people who were involved. The immediate support of a roommate was so very good!

We politely avoided the subject of religion, at first, although it seemed Ann, too, had been reading the Bible, particularly passages from some of the prophets and the New Testament. She asked if I knew when Ash Wednesday was. Chagrined, I told her about my attempt to get a message through. So much for the reliability of our "hostesses." They had not delivered a prayer book I had sent to Ann, either, although they had assured me she had said thank you for it.

St. Patrick's Day was upon us. We were still receiving Christmas cards, and when I started to discard the envelopes, Ann stopped me. "Don't throw those colored envelopes out! We can make shamrocks out of the green." We obtained permission to put two in the bathroom, and we used the rest to add to our gallery of greeting cards taped to the walls of our room.

Then it was *No Ruz*, the Iranian New Year. This is roughly the equivalent of Christmas and New Year's, and it falls on the first day of spring. It is celebrated for nearly a week. Houses are cleaned, special food is prepared, and almost everyone gets new clothes. Gifts are also exchanged. The year before, I had celebrated *No Ruz* at the home of my Farsi teacher in Washington. The table there was decorated lavishly and laden with traditional Iranian food. Quite a contrast to the hospitality here.

"Let's make gifts for them," Ann suggested. "I pressed the narcissus I got. We can use them to make bookmarks." She mounted a pressed flower on a slip of paper and in my very best script I wrote "Happy Iranian New Year, March 21, 1980, American Embassy, Tehran." Accompanied by sticks of gum, these were our *No Ruz* gifts to our guards. Fortunately we made plenty, because those who weren't on duty came to wish their friends "Happy New Year" and to pick up *their* bookmark.

Later, Ann and I talked about what to do for Easter. We

122

had sent each other Valentines, and I had received her New Year's hat and card. Could we do something to encourage the guys? While our plans were still in the talking stage, we started saving odds and ends. Ann never discarded envelopes, and after her arrival I saw the wisdom of keeping those colored pieces of paper.

We began to scavenge other things, too, from the wastepaper basket in the bathroom: plastic detergent bottles, toilet paper tubes, caps from used toothpaste tubes, jars— anything that would be handy. We became expert rag pickers and pack rats, both of us.

About two weeks before Easter, the captors began grooming us for the "Easter Show." Mail arrived with fair regularity, meaning about once a week, and we were given a box of books one of my friends had sent. The books were about the Person and work of the Holy Spirit. Ann, it seemed, had been reading, thinking, and questioning for several months now, too; and at last, here was something to sink our spiritual teeth into.

The day those books came, we were also permitted to select a large number of volumes from the library located in the basement of the warehouse, known since the February, 1979, revolution as "The Mushroom Inn." We had been taken there to shower and were allowed to go into the room set up as a library and actually select books—quite a contrast from the shopping cart full that usually came around! We felt so rich. With this huge reading selection in front of us, we each picked a book that dealt with the renewal movement in the Christian church. There was not a sound in our room all day as we read in great big thirsty gulps. What a treat! We read and read, stopped and talked briefly, read again and talked some more about what we had read. We each finished our books, and then swapped them and started over again.

Holy Week was a time of deep study and prayer. We reveled in the books that had come our way and our chance to talk about them. We were still doing that sort of dance that people do, trying to figure out how the other was think-

123

ing. We didn't talk about our developing friendship; we let our relationship in Christ build very slowly. Independently we had each decided to observe Sundays with special worship and rest. Now we added "family devotions" each evening as we shared a Scripture reading, the singing of a hymn, and prayer for our families and for the Christian community. It seemed the Spirit had to work quietly in each of us before we were ready to reach out and work with each other.

Easter was close at hand. On Good Friday, I fasted again. This brought more questions from the girls, and they seemed infinitely relieved when I reached for breakfast on Saturday morning. I believe now, with the usual 20/20 vision of hindsight, that a hunger strike would have absolutely terrified them.

Saturday we were blindfolded and driven to the ambassador's residence where we were led to a walled-in garden off the ambassador's kitchen for our occasional airing out. There was an abundance of ivy growing on the garden walls, and we picked some to carry back inside. We would have green plants growing in our room. Inspired, we also picked up colorful bits of tile and stones from the grounds. We could put them in the bottom of our jam jars to make planters.

Though these times in the garden so far had been brief, usually no longer than twenty minutes every week or so since St. Patrick's Day, it was a glorious chance to be outside, to see the treetops, the sky, some birds, and maybe later in the year, glimpse a flower.

I was busy collecting ivy when I became aware the sister was staring at me intently. "You really hate Iran and the Iranian people, don't you?" she said suddenly.

"Is that what you want me to say?" I asked, still gathering greenery.

"No. But you must hate us!" she said softly.

"I can't," I responded and turned to face her. "I don't like what you are doing. I think you are wrong, and this action won't solve a thing. But I don't hate you."

124

"Just give the Shah back and you can go home," she said.

"It's more than the Shah, isn't it? What would happen if he did come back?"

"He would be tried and executed. He must pay for his crimes."

"If he dies, who will that bring back? What will his death accomplish?" I asked.

"He must pay for his crimes."

It was another dead-end conversation. I turned and walked to the other end of the garden.

I thought about that interlude as Ann and I began to plan how we would use the fresh greenery to decorate for Easter. That symbol of life would be used for sure!

We spread our scrounged treasures on the floor and decided to make Easter baskets first. We had salvaged two plastic detergent bottles and started with them.

"Could we have a pair of scissors?" I asked. I could never remember the Farsi word for scissors, and to compensate, I had become quite adept at body language: I was making a cutting motion with my fingers. Amazingly, the scissors came.

We cut the bottles down to basket size, leaving two long narrow strips on each side which we could fold to make a handle. A needle and thread made it possible to stitch the handles together.

We had nothing to color the bottles with, so out came the colored envelopes we had saved. I used blue, cut it to size, folded it around the plastic, and taped it in place. Pink trim made a ribbon, and there it was: an Easter basket. Ann made a similar one decorated in green and yellow.

Now we needed some eggs. I thought a minute and reached into my desk drawer. "These are funny looking eggs, Ann," I commented, handing her a packet of small assorted Christmas tree ornaments. "But they will fill our baskets." We used the white, gold, and red balls. The blue ones we left tucked away in the desk for another day.

125

Then we started to create animals. I worked on the chicks, and Ann made a small lamb and two Easter rabbits. They weren't masterpieces, but they marched across our radiator with gay bravado.

The basic material for all of these animals was the cardboard tubes from toilet paper rolls. The students kept us well supplied with pastel-colored toilet papers from the embassy co-op, and it was from there we secured enough paper for our yellow chicks, blue bunnies, and pink lamb. A pink top from a detergent bottle made a perfect sized basket for the rabbit—we sat him on the mirror shelf in the bathroom— and an unpopped pistachio nut made just the right shaped egg. (We must have replaced that "egg" a half dozen times.)

The guards were fascinated by what we were doing, and they watched closely as we wrapped, cut, pinched, poked, and glued to come up with each creation. As a matter of fact, they brought the other girls in just to see our decorations.

My sister Micki had copied virtually the entire Lenten and Easter section from the *Lutheran Book of Prayer* for me, ending each of her letters with a different prayer. So, we would have Easter prayers with our worship service, along with our Bibles and hymns. We could celebrate Easter, the resurrection of Jesus Christ, along with all the rest of Christendom.

We were taken off for a bath on Saturday afternoon, a privilege we cherished and nearly dreaded at the same time. Bathrooms and tubs often were almost beyond description. The dirt, and grime would have been a challenge for any cleanser. Ann and I usually had to spend more of our precious minutes cleaning the tub or shower than we got to spend cleaning ourselves.

Holidays were always occasions for baths in Iran, but it also could mean we would be having company! Ann and I harbored a secret hope that, if visitors came, the students would shovel the garbage out of the hallways. Plastic bags of leftover food, toilet paper, and other throwaways had been piling up for weeks on end. When the garbage was carted off, we took that as a sign a visitor was coming.

126

I had deliberately planned ahead so my dress would be clean; I was determined to dress up for Easter the best I could. And I would have a cross. The little gold cross I was wearing when I was kidnapped had been taken from me, with the rest of my jewelry, in late November. But during Lent, a packet and a letter had arrived from Mary Jane. "Katie," she explained, "the congregation at Messiah Lutheran wants you to have one of their Lenten crosses." Messiah Lutheran was a church I had been a member of in Alexandria, Virginia. I put it on immediately and wore it continuously, another link to home.

I had gotten into the habit of lying down at 5:00 P.M. for a quick nap. And that Saturday, after expending energy cleaning the room and having a hot shower, I was feeling particularly sleepy. I rolled up in a blanket for a quick forty winks. I had just dropped off when there was a knock at the door, and one of the brothers stuck his head in.

"Oh, she's asleep. I'll come back later," he said.

"No!" Ann and I said simultaneously.

"I was just dozing. I'm awake," I said.

"Well, these are from your friends," he said, thrusting two plastic bags at us. We were flabbergasted!

"Thank you. Merci!" was all we could say. Each sack contained a shirt, some undies, soap, shampoo, deodorant, toothpaste and a toothbrush, and a note which read "From Your Diplomatic Colleagues."

Our bedtime had moved later and later into the evening, but we puttered about on that Saturday night more than usual. Ann was still working when I finally put my bed down and turned in. She continued to read and fuss under her breath, and I wondered if she was upset about not being home. So much good had happened since we had become roommates. We supported each other. We talked; we exchanged ideas. I was exercising more. But I could understand her missing her family. Though she did not have the bevy of sisters I did, I knew she had a close family circle.

I finally fell asleep. The next morning when I awoke my eye fell on something sitting on our desk. It was a stone on a piece of green paper, and on that stone a small wooden cross. The cross was made of two pieces of wood tied together with thread, and it was stuck on the rock with chewing gum.

"Kate, you talk about the Rock so much, and the imagery of the rock is important in all your worship," Ann explained. "I thought you'd *never* go to sleep so I could get that made." So this was what she had been trying to do the night before!

That lowly, thoughtful Easter gift promptly became the centerpiece for our worship altar for the duration of our stay. What a symbol of the strong place, the solid rock, the fortress that our Lord Jesus is.

I did not have a gift for Ann, so when she went off to brush her teeth I flew to work. I thought fast and made a special bookmark for her and slipped it into her Bible. She found it a couple days later. Then I put an Easter card I had received into a recycled envelope and placed it by her Easter basket, ready for her to find.

At about noon we held our Easter worship service. Thank God for the hymnal and our Bibles! We prayed together, using the prayers Micki had copied for us. I could hardly pray them, I was so choked up. I knew my family would be using them, too.

Later, there was a festive meal of turkey, mashed potatoes, and cranberry sauce. The air was charged with expectancy. Something was happening!

In the afternoon it came.

"You are going to see the priest. Put on your blindfolds." We were led out of the room.

By this time, Ann and I were very good at moving about together blindfolded. She would follow me with one hand on my shoulder, and the sister would guide me by taking my elbow.

Through the hall we went. "Watch out for the double door," I warned. Half of it was usually closed. "Don't trip on the brother's feet that are stuck out in the middle of the corridor." There were always guards—and guns—in the hall.

128

The front door of the embassy must be open: There is a lot of light. Left. Turn. Up steps. Fourteen. A landing. Fourteen more steps. Use the handrail. Lots of people in the corridor. Are we here?

As our blindfolds came off, I tried not to gag at the sight of what had been done to the walls of the hallway. Slogans were *painted* everywhere. Into the deputy chief of mission's office we went. There were candy, cakes, posters of Khomeini, red crepe paper, TV cameras, and male students everywhere. But *none* of our colleagues. We were not to see them this holiday either! At least one of the men looked like an American. Was it Bishop Gumbleton again? *No*, I thought, as I met him with my hand outstretched.

"Hello, I'm Reverend Bremer from Lawrence, Kansas. How are you?"

We talked a bit, and then I moved from Pastor Bremer to the man standing behind the table. Ann whispered that one man, Monsignor Anibale Bugnini, was the papal nuncio, and I recognized Archbishop Capudji. We exchanged greetings. For a moment Monsignor Bugnini and I were left unguarded. "Did you get the shirts?" he asked.

"Yes, thank you! Those packages were wonderful!" I said.

"I took shirts to Laingen and the others at the Foreign Ministry, too," he said.

"When?" The question was breathless. Ann and I had often speculated on the fate of Bruce, Mike, and Vic.

"Yesterday," came the reply.

"How are they?"

"Fine."

Our conversation was cut off as we moved into more general contact with the rest of those present. Then, one of the ministers called us to order. We held hands in a small circle, and Pastor Bremer began to pray.

"We thank You that on this day the human darkness is pierced by the brightness of Easter morning. We thank You that the light of that resurrection shines into this place of

129

confinement and into the hearts of these, our sisters and brothers. We ask that You be in the hearts of the Iranian people and in the hearts of the American people, and that Your light will lead us to a new friendship together and justice.

"Now we ask that Your special blessing may be here upon Ann and Kate, and that You will fill them with a sense of Your presence and Your Spirit. For the sake of Jesus Christ, our Lord and Savior who both died and lives for us. Let us all say together, Amen."

I raised my head, amazed. The Lord had just answered one of my questions. I had wondered so often *how* to pray for the Ayatollah and the leaders of Iran. Now Pastor Bremer had prayed that the love and light of God would so fill Iran that *God's* will would be done. Here was my answer.

The archbishop finally said, "Please, sit down." Ann and I did, facing a large TV camera. "I told the students I would come only if I could bring you messages from your family, and take messages back to them," he went on.

We began to answer questions about our personal welfare and what we were doing in our "spare time." Then the archbishop called for the "envelopes." What was this?

He handed Ann an envelope, and then one to me. A letter from our families! I was so nervous I could hardly see the printing on the page. When I had an opportunity in a few minutes to speak to my family via that TV camera, it was obvious nothing had registered. I had no idea I should answer their one question: Why had they had no letter from me for weeks? I was writing regularly three times a week—all I was permitted—and I should have said so!

Instead I faced the camera squarely and said, "The only reason I'm losing weight, Mother, is that I decided that was the one thing I could do while I was here." Ann and I both talked about our daily routines, getting to bed late, both being night owls, reading, exercising. The excitement of it all had made us giddy, and we laughed and giggled like two schoolgirls.

130

"Which one of you keeps the other in good spirits?" Pastor Bremer asked, smiling. Neither Ann nor I said a thing, but simply pointed to each other!

After the TV coverage, we moved over to a couch that faced a coffee table covered with candy bars, brownies, nuts, cakes, and one enormous, red-wrapped Easter egg. We were given plastic bags and encouraged to take plenty. The students were busy telling the archbishop about the library they had set up, the exercise room where we could play ping-pong (we had done so twice), and the videotapes of American films they were showing us (we had seen one).

Pastor Bremer said he could not talk about political matters, but he added, "You're both very important people back home." Ann and I did not understand what he meant, for we had no idea how involved the whole nation had become with the hostage crisis. But we did understand the American people were aware that something was going on, and we were grateful for that.

All too soon we were led back to our room. We had been given a packet of mail, so we sorted it out, answered the sisters' questions about the "Easter party," and reread those precious bits of mail that the archbishop had brought.

It must have been 11:30 in the evening when one of the brothers stopped by to tell us the ministers had said, "The women were the best adjusted of the hostages." Ann and I wondered at the compliment, but having worked through discriminatory practices in our earlier years in the foreign service, we were glad to hear we were bearing up well in comparison with our male colleagues. It also made us wonder what kind of treatment the men were receiving.*

As we calmed down, the realization began to set in that we had been used for propaganda. I didn't know whether I was sorry or happy about that. We had been given an opportunity to let our families know we were all right, but we had

_____
*After our release, it became evident that some of them had been treated quite harshly.

131

played right into the students' hands with our smiling faces and amusing chatter. We talked about it and determined that if the opportunity came for us to be televised again, it would definitely be with a more serious demeanor.

By now we were hungry.

"Excuse me, sister." I said to one of the girls. "Where is supper?"

"I'll see." She left the room and came back in a few moments to announce there was only bread, cheese, and dates.

"Is there any tea?" I asked.

"Yes. I'll bring some. Give me your glasses." She picked them up and returned in short order with tea, bread, cheese, and dates. It was all fresh and good, a lovely ending to a beautiful Easter.

Ann and I bowed our heads and gave thanks for all of the blessings of the day. We asked the Lord to keep our families. And we settled down to wait for yet another day.

Hostage rescue mission fails/
Daring attempt foiled
by equipment failure
Des Moines Register
April 25, 1980

10

APRIL, 1980

The euphoria from Easter lasted several days. Ann and I had received mail, and we had had a chance to say something to our families. Our room was almost pretty. We had taped an assortment of greeting cards to the walls—birds and flowers here, water and sailing there. We even had a family grouping in one corner: pictures of my parents, nieces, and nephews and of Ann's mother and godchildren.

In my corner I had a little altar arrangement, a mix of Easter and Christmas cards. My nephew Mark's confirmation classmates had sent cross-shaped greeting cards, and I taped these across the wall above my bed. The room was painted in a yellow tone, the curtains were bright green, the carpet nondescript. But with the greeting cards it had become home.

"Hahnum Koob, what are these?" asked one of the sisters on duty, pointing to some homemade cards from Messiah Lutheran.

"They are cards made by children where I went to church when I lived in America," I answered.

"They are funny. Why are the eggs in a cage?"

The card showed a picture of two decorated eggs in a cage. "The eggs are a symbol of the resurrection, the reason

133

we celebrate Easter. New life comes from the egg, just as we believe Christ died and rose again."

"But why the cage?"

"I'm not sure," I said. "Perhaps the boy was trying to tell us that without His new life we are still boxed in." (My private thoughts were that it was his personal reference to our status!)

Our pack rat natures got busy again. Ann and I had been given a set of checkers and chessmen, which the students had rifled from the embassy co-op. I had a square piece of wood from the previous room I had occupied, which I was using as a lap board for writing and playing solitaire.

We measured and drew and double-checked with a dictionary definition of checkers to make sure our colors were correct. We had ourselves a checkerboard. Then I dredged up what I could remember from the little chess I had played in college days, and we even played chess. I never had been much of a game player, but anything to help pass time! We also made up some new rules and played a sort of two-handed bridge.

One night shortly after Easter, several of the girls came into the room while we were doing our exercises. It must have looked like a woman's gym class as we went through our various calisthenic routines. Ann and I demonstrated our favorites to the girls, and in some instances even challenged them to a difficult routine. But the girls had an unfair advantage: They were twenty years younger!

Things were going well. The sisters were attentive and agreeable. We were permitted baths on a regular schedule (about every six days), visits to the garden for twenty minutes before baths, and we had green plants, cards, books, and of course, our daily devotions.

Abruptly, there was a change. Hamid arrived in a rage.

"Why do you think the sisters have no authority? The women are just like us. You must not treat them like servants," he said.

"What do you mean?" Ann asked, completely taken aback.

134

"They are not your servants. They work with us for the revolution. They are important in our work here. If you have problems, talk to the sisters, and they will take care of it," Hamid said.

"Look, we would love to make our own tea and do our own laundry. But you've said that we are your guests and are not permitted to do these things. So we ask the sisters for the things we need—water, tea, trips to the bathroom. We do not consider them servants," I chimed in.

The conversation continued for a few minutes.

"What did we do that made them think we are treating them as servants?" Ann asked after Hamid left.

We talked about it not only between ourselves but with the girls. No clues. The only problem we could imagine was that occasionally late at night one of the girls would come in drinking a cup of tea, and we would ask if there was tea for us, too. Usually they would not come into the room eating or drinking unless they could offer us something, too. That is, except for Queenie and Princess, who inevitably showed up late at night to sit and drink tea in front of us.

We discussed the tea issue with some of the sisters and asked them to let us know if we had offended them. We pointed out that as adult women we certainly should be able to discuss what bothered us and settle our differences without the interference of the brothers. Nothing further was ever mentioned.

Except once. It was April 12. We woke up as usual, shortly before ten o'clock, and started in with our usual routine. I got up, wrapped the blanket around me sarong style, and asked if I could go to the toilet.

"I'll see," said the ever-present sister.

She was new to morning duty, so Ann said, "You'll have to tell the brothers to put our name on the list so we can use the bathroom."

She left the room and returned very quickly. "It isn't empty," she said. This was her way of saying no. Then she smiled and said, "He'll come when you can use it."

135

"Please," Ann said. "Tell him that we are up and want to use the bathroom."

Her smile soured a bit. "I've told you he will come." We settled down to wait. We heard the hourly time tone on the radio. Ten o'clock.

Ann whispered to me, "I'm going to see how long this takes."

We waited patiently, growing more and more uncomfortable. Finally we heard the eleven o'clock time tone on the radio.

"*Hohar*,"* I finally said to the sister. "It's been over an hour. Can't you please find out if we can use the bathroom or go downstairs to another one?"

She had been writing busily. She looked up, about to refuse. Then she left the room. Again, she came back quickly. "It's empty. You can go."

"Go ahead, Ann," I said. "I think I can wait a bit."

Ann left and came back in very short order.

I handed the sister my blindfold and picked up my dress, toothbrush, toothpaste, towel, and washcloth as I had been doing for four months and moved toward the door.

"You must get dressed before you can go," the sister announced.

"Excuse me," I said. "This is how I have dressed to go to the bathroom for four months. The robe is too short so I use the blanket. Let's go."

"I'll ask the brother," she said. She left the room and returned almost at once. "You may have done so in the past, but you won't anymore!" she declared triumphantly.

"Sister, either you take me to the bathroom now, or I'm going on my own. I have waited for over an hour, and you refused to do anything about it. I can't wait to change clothes. I need to go now!" I was angry, and my voice was low and hard.

She flounced across the room.

---

*Farsi for "sister."

I reached for the door and was in the hall before she could stop me. As I headed briskly down the corridor, I saw one of the smallest of the brothers at the other end. There were two or three more brothers seated on the couches and chairs along the way, but all I could see was the minute Ali. He was much smaller than I, and he knew I was angry. He was absolutely amazed to see me alone.

"I'm going to the toilet," I explained curtly, turned to the bathroom, knocked, and entered.

I was busy washing up when the sister came bursting through the bathroom door. I don't believe I have ever seen such hatred as there was in her dark, deep-set eyes. She was so mad she could not speak.

I took one look at her and spat out, "Sister, enough is enough!" Then I calmed down. "I'm sorry I left the room. I know it was wrong. But I had to go to the bathroom."

She still did not speak. I finished washing and gathered up my things. We marched back to the room together, I with my blindfold tightly in place.

The incident was followed by an interminable round of discussions with the brothers and the sisters that day. I knew they would have to punish me. I just hoped they wouldn't take it out on Ann. She had done nothing. Would they separate us? That was my worst fear.

I tried to sort out my jumbled thoughts in my morning devotions. What I had done was dangerous and foolish. There were guns in that corridor, no matter how hard I tried to ignore them. The sister abitrarily changed the rules, and under the circumstances I refused to buy it. But she was the jailer; I was the hostage.

"Dear Lord, help me to accept what comes. And don't let me do anything so foolish again," I prayed.

Round and round my thoughts ran. *It was certainly the most exciting thing that has happened since Easter*, I rationalized to myself.

Several of the sisters showed up at our door. "Miss Koob," said one. "We certainly never expected this of you. We thought you had more respect for our customs."

137

"And I thought you were concerned about our physical well-being," I retorted. "I needed to go to the bathroom."

Zahro came in the room. "You were both a little wrong," she said calmly. *That is the most appropriate thing I've heard all day*, I thought, as a regular stream of visitors arrived, each to hear for herself the "true story." Zahro was kind, but I had no doubt where her loyalties lay.

Over and over again, Ann and I recited how we had asked the sister for permission to go to the bathroom, how we had told her what she must do, how she had ignored us for over an hour, how she had finally refused to take me because she didn't like the way I was dressed (though I had been going to the bathroom in the mornings dressed that way for over four months), how I had told her I would go myself if she wouldn't take me, and on and on and on.

"Miss Koob," said one of the brothers who stopped by. "That was very foolish. You could have been shot, you know."

"I know I was wrong," I said. "But so was the sister. I had to use the toilet."

"But couldn't you have taken the few minutes to change? You must do what the sisters tell you."

"No, I couldn't wait," I rebutted.

"If you had waited that long, surely you could have waited a few more minutes," he insisted.

The discussions continued endlessly.

About 5:00 P.M. two of the sisters entered the room. They were nervous—and smiling. "Get your things together. You're moving."

So this was it. Where would we go?

"Will we need to wear our coats?" Ann asked.

"No."

We began putting our things into our pillowcases. I used my cape as a tote bag. Two of the brothers arrived, and one mattress left with them. We said we needed the heater, the lamp, our books. We sorted the books we used every day, our Bibles, the hymnal, our devotional books, and put them into the bags we intended to carry.

Blindfolds on and into the corridor. We walked too far to

138

be going downstairs. Upstairs? Up the main staircase to the next level. The air was stifling.

Off with the blindfolds. We were in a room that had no window. Unsightly pieces of what had once been draperies were nailed over doors on each side of the room. There wasn't a breath of air to be found anywhere.

"General Gast's office!" mumbled Ann. I had never been there before, but it was *hot*. We surveyed our surroundings. One very suspicious looking "mattress" turned out to be a piece of foam rubber and the remains of a box spring. There was also one good mattress carried up from our room.

"Ann, this is my fault. You take the good mattress," I said.

"We're in this together," she said firmly. "We'll share."

"OK," I said, "but you start with the good one." And so it was agreed.

The room was almost unbearable but that turned out to be a blessing. The sisters were hotter than we were, so they began keeping guard duty outside. We were alone!

We soon decided the change in rooms wasn't just because I had "run." We were not responding to captivity the way they had expected. We had made our adjustments and were too happy to be good hostages. In fact, we were almost acting like the girls were *our* guests, sharing our candy and gum from the co-op. So we "needed" to be reminded that we were under their control. I only knew that we were not coping well because of our own strength. Again we were reminded we were being supported and sustained by the Lord.

With this in mind, we purposely determined that our new room and its heightened deprivation was not going to change our attitude, our routines, or our behavior toward the sisters.

We set about decorating and cleaning. We had salvaged a number 10 tin can one night when we were the last to receive fruit cocktail for dessert, and the bathroom had detergent. We found some rags and set about scrubbing the walls, sweeping out the dirt, and putting up the tinsel.

139

My worship corner went up above the head of my bed. Leftover tinsel from Christmas was draped over the thermostat, and our Easter baskets and handcrafted menagerie were set in order across a non-working radiator. The heater arrived (I only wished we needed it!) and so did the lamp. We were home.

Being in a room with no windows distorted our sense of time, and though meal service continued regularly, not being able to see the changing light was disorienting. We became more and more dependent on the watch we had been given.

A blessing, we assumed, would be no mosquitos, but they found us anyway. They thrive year-round in Tehran. But with no window, the noise of the demonstrations from the street was definitely muted.

We had been in our new habitat only two days when we were ushered off to the room where our Easter celebration had been held. We were told representatives of the Red Cross wanted to speak with us.

Two men were there to meet us, one tall and dark-haired, the other a short, gray-haired man who was introduced to us in French as a medical doctor. The taller of the two had a clipboard and was the spokesman. Several brothers clustered around us, shoving a running tape recorder under our noses.

"Aren't we supposed to be able to meet with you privately?" Ann asked.

"Under normal circumstances, yes," the man said. "But we are fortunate to be here at all. We have been promised we will see all of you. We are the first visitors allowed to see everyone. Others have seen only some of you."

My eyes were scanning the clipboard, trying not to be too obvious. The students watched us very closely.

"We'd like to know how you are," the man said. "Are you being treated OK? Are you getting outside? Do you get to exercise? Is your room big enough? How about your meals?"

A big list. I looked at Ann and she at me.

"We had a lovely room until two days ago," she said.

140

"Now we are in a room that has no window and no ventilation."

"No ventilation!" he exclaimed.

The Red Cross representative was explaining the situation to the doctor in French. I could hear the students talking to each other and muttering, "But that's their own fault. They did it to themselves."

He turned to us again. Almost as if by rote I said, "The students try to meet all of our physical needs: toothpaste, soap, and other things like that. We exercise in our room, but we only get outside about once a week."

"How about your meals?" I thought I heard him say. He was obviously pressed for time. This interview was going to be short, but that was fine if they saw all of us.

"The meals are more than adequate. The cook is very good . . ." I began.

"No, not food, I mean your *mail*, letters from your family and friends," he corrected.

"We don't get much," I said.

"It has been months since I've had a letter from my mother," Ann added.

"What about the Red Cross messages?" he asked.

"We have received none. We were given forms, once, to mail in November," I recalled.

He handed us duplicate forms and said,"Here. These will go to your parents." We felt quite sure they would. Pens were provided, and we wrote swiftly and signed our names. The interviews were over.

Back in our room with the door closed, we compared notes.

"Did you see the list?" I asked.

"No," said Ann. "The angle was wrong."

"I remember seeing Barry's name and Bill's. But I didn't see John Graves's or Mike's. I wonder where they are?"

"It makes me so mad we couldn't see them without the brothers," Ann complained. "That contravenes all international protocol that the Red Cross works with. Even in Vietnam, and here, before the Shah fell, they saw political prisoners privately!"

"Did you hear the guys telling them it was our fault we are in this room?" I asked.

"No. Did they?"

"When we started talking about the heat and no window, they started murmuring to each other. You can bet they'll figure some way to let those two men know we're dangerous," I said.

Two days later we were told to put on our blindfolds once again. Down to the interview room once more. We were there for about an hour, looking at a video episode of "Little House on the Prairie." Then it was back to our room.

When we arrived, there was a slight commotion going on. We stepped inside the room apprehensively, took off our blindfolds, and there, at the top of what had been the bricked-in window, was a hole. The students had decided we should have air, and had removed some bricks and knocked out one pane of glass. It was glorious. We could see treetops and sky again, and it did let a measure of fresh air into the room. The grin on the face of the brother seemed genuine when he saw our smiles of relief.

"This is better, no?" he asked.

"Absolutely!" we chorused, ignoring the plaster dust. "Thank you!"

Ann came back from the bathroom one morning with a strange look on her face. She sat down carefully, silently warning me not to say anything. The sister left.

"Kate," she breathed. "Look!" She reached inside her shirt and pulled out a letter. It was three pages of typewritten script addressed to her, and it had been torn in half and thrown away. She found it in the wastebasket in the john.

A sound was heard at the door. Quick, hide the letter. Lunch came. Room service left. We were too excited to eat.

Ann read quickly, silently. It was a letter from her cousin. It was, she said, written for the benefit of the students. He talked about the Shah's move to Egypt from Panama and how no one had much chance of stopping a man with his kind of money and contacts. In this way, we had new clues as to what was going on in the outside world. She showed the letter to me, but I was too nervous and excited for much of it to register.

Now the question was, what to do with the letter. She put it back in the trash where she had found it, and we prayed that someone else would see it. That night we thanked God for the news and for family contact for Ann.

Our days seemed filled with distractions as we coped with our slightly ventilated "sauna room." The students were allowing us to see videotapes twice a week now, and we were curled up on the sofa in the video room watching a Western one afternoon when the door burst open without warning. Hamid came in, followed by another student and Mullah Khameni, the leader of Friday prayers at the university. We stumbled to our feet, pulled down our shirt tails, and checked our cuffs and buttons.

"*Salamm,*" we said as our greeting.

"*Salamm alechim,*" he answered. He continued on in Farsi. "How are you?"

"Fine, thank you, and you?" we replied with the formula taught us in the first Farsi lesson.

Hamid explained that the mullah had come to see if we were OK, if we needed anything, and if the students were treating us well. I deferred to Ann.

"We are in good physical health, thank you. The students try to provide us with the things we need for our physical wants, but we are always afraid." She spoke in English.

Hamid translated. "They say they are all right. The students take good care of them. But they are always a little nervous."

"Excuse me," Ann interrupted in Farsi, "I did not say nervous. I said afraid."

Everyone was silent.

The mullah finally broke the strained quiet. "I'm glad to

143

hear the students are treating you well. As soon as the United States government releases the Shah, you will be on your way home. We hope that can happen soon. It is your government's fault you are still here."

It was useless for us to respond to his political rhetoric, so we let the comment pass and the mullah left. We sat back down and resumed watching the video.

After we had returned to the room, the sister we called Tiger Lily appeared.* "Why did you say you were afraid?" she began.

"Because we are," Ann said bluntly. "You told us after Kate went to the bathroom by herself that she was lucky she wasn't shot. You sit outside our doors with guns."

"We'd be fools not to be afraid," I broke in.

"We never know when you will come through that door and tell us we are going to trial, or that we already have been tried," added Ann. "We are afraid all the time, every day. We live with fear."

By most terrorist standards, they had been kind. However, that didn't alter the fact that we lived facing fear and death each day. We had learned to accommodate those feelings and take them before the Lord. But our fears were real and had to be considered.

It was not long after this conversation that our fears were heightened anew. I went off for my regular trip to the bathroom, but I returned white as a sheet.

"Ann," I said almost in tears, closing the door carefully, "I'm afraid someone has flipped out."

"What do you mean?" she asked. She stopped her reading to look up. My heart was palpitating with fear.

"I was sitting blindfolded on the sofa waiting for my turn to use the toilet. There was someone else sitting beside me—American. He could hardly talk.

"He sounded like a three-year-old. All he could say was 'Bathroom? My turn? Bathroom.' It was horrible." I started to cry. "I've never heard such a voice."

---

*Most Americans knew her as "Mary," the students' spokesperson.

"Kate, are you sure?" Ann asked.

"Really. I was so scared. I don't know who he was or why he talked that way. But this person sounded as if he'd been reduced to the mentality of a child."

We were both quiet. What was going on? I never learned who the man was, nor did I hear any further details from the guards. But the little scene was alarming, and one more trauma with which we had to cope.

We had been in the hot box two weeks, almost to the day, when the sisters were aflutter again. They were like so many excited wrens as they flitted in and out of our room, all atwitter with whispers, the secretive smiles back on their faces. They could hardly suppress the excitement they were feeling, and it increased as the day wore on. They would come in, look at us, and leave almost as if they were afraid they would say something. When we thought we had just about had it with the fun and games, one of the girls came in with the now familiar announcement.

"Get your things ready. We're moving you."

"Do we take everything?" I asked.

"Pack just what you need. The other things, leave on the mattress. We'll bring them to you," the sister said.

"We've heard that one before," I muttered.

Ann and I moved around the room, filling our plastic bags with things we really wanted and sorting out the books into first and second priorities. We knew we'd lose something on this move, too.

Hamid entered the room. "You can't take much," he warned. "Just what you need."

"Where are we going?" I asked.

"Perhaps on a long trip." He grinned at us.

"Hamid, are we going home?" I asked imprudently.

There was no answer, just dancing eyes and a look that *could* have meant yes.

"Don't get your hopes up," warned Ann when the sister and brother left the room.

"I'm not really," I said. "But it would be nice."

We had started packing about 6:30 P.M. Finally we were

145

ready, and we sat down to wait. Eight-thirty . . . still no dinner. "You'll get dinner at your new place," Hamid had said.

Ten-thirty. We were still waiting.

Ann knocked at the door. "Can we please have something to eat?" We had already dug into our store of chocolate saved from Easter and the nuts we hoarded from our meals. "They have assumed the responsibility to feed us, and they can't get away with this," she said to me, pounding the door again. "We are hungry. It's late. We'd like some food."

The sister finally showed up with two bowls of chili con carne, and we ate ravenously. As we finished, we could hear the tramp of heavy feet in the corridor and men talking in Farsi.

I banged on the door. "Sister, I'd like to go to the bathroom."

One of the girls opened the door, and I picked up the soup bowls to wash just as she was ready to put on my blindfold. "Can you find me a glass, Ann? I'd like some water," I said. She reached into our packs and put a glass into my waiting hand. As I followed the sister down the hall, my blindfold was slipping loose, and I could see a bit. Blankets tied up like camper's bundles were everywhere. *Everyone* was being moved, not just us. It wasn't because our sentence in the hot box was over. Something was afoot!

I washed the bowls, was re-blindfolded, and returned with the sister to our now bare room. I told Ann what I had seen, and she decided to see if she could get a peek for herself. Back she came, confirming my report.

While she was out of the room, I pulled Corrie ten Boom's *Tramp for the Lord* from my pack and started to read. The book moved quickly, and I didn't want to leave it behind partially finished. It was filled with the triumph of faith every step of the way and was so encouraging.

The night grew later and later. No action. Finally, about 12:30, one of the sisters came in. "Plans have changed. We won't move you tonight. You can sleep here," she said.

146

"You've already got our blankets and sheets. Can we have them back?" I asked. They brought each of us a sheet and a blanket, and I went off to the toilet again to wash my face and brush my teeth.

"You'll be sorry if you go to sleep," warned Ann when I returned.

"Probably," I agreed. "But I'm bushed. If I'm asleep at least I won't be angry about sitting around waiting. I wonder," I added for the fifteenth time, "where in the world they will take us!"

I rolled up in my blanket and turned toward the wall. Ann picked up *Tramp for the Lord*.

Suddenly the sisters were in the room. "Let's go!"

Ann looked at me and grinned, and I returned her glance with an appropriate grimace. We picked up our blankets and sheets and grabbed our Bibles, the hymnal, Thomas à Kempis' *Imitation of Christ*, and the goodie bags we had set aside. We turned our backs to the girls, and they tied our blindfolds firmly in place.

Forty-two steps down the hall. Turn. A few more steps. Grab the handrail. Down fourteen steps, a landing, down twelve steps, another landing. A turn, but a surprise: not to the right, to the left. *We are not leaving the building.*

We moved through a maze of obstacles and finally were dumped into a room that was about as dirty as any we had been in the whole time. Evidently three people had been living there, for there were three bed rolls and three sets of dirty linen and stacks of books. In one corner, written in a vertical column, were the words KHOMEINI HILTON 176 DAYS. Someone else was counting! And someone else thought they might be going home.

We shuffled things around, claimed a mattress each, and fell asleep. Cleaning up could wait till morning.

April 26, 1980. Unknowingly we had lived through the tragedy of the rescue attempt.

**Iran disperses hostages/
Vows to return bodies
of 8 U.S. commandos**
Des Moines Register
April 26, 1980

11

SPRING, 1980

The morning light of April 26 brought a new day, and Ann and I set about to appraise our situation. This room needed *cleaning*!

We started out with rags and water, asked for the vacuum cleaner and swept, and scrubbed away several months' worth of accumulated dirt. We liked the room, for it was bright and airy, and it was on the back side of the embassy away from the noise.

We did wonder briefly if we had properly ascertained our location, for twice shortly after we moved we were awakened at 2:45 A.M. by heavy gunfire. And it sounded as if it was originating *on* the compound. We were extremely frightened, and the students wouldn't tell us what was happening. Ann and I tried to decide if or where, in our skimpily furnished room, we could hide.

We were in this room only about two weeks when Hamid came in and said, "Get your things ready. We are moving you." We were not completely surprised. Shortly after we had everything clean, another of the brothers had come in, looked the room over, and nodded his head approvingly.

"Hamid," I asked, "can't we just go clean the other room for you? We like this room!"

148

"It is not possible," he replied. "You think we only want you to clean rooms?"

Obediently, Ann and I put our things together and moved to another room just across the hall. We were back on the street side, and this room was dirty, too. Into the scrub bucket one more time.

We could hear the demonstrations on the street outside our window clearly now, but we could also hear the noises of everyday normal traffic: taxis, buses, automobiles, and pedestrians. They were so close, and yet we were so isolated.

The guards became less obnoxious about our having papers and pencils, so I decided to keep a diary on the back of used envelopes, which I then tucked away safely inside my Bible. I had realized I couldn't keep dates and events in my head any longer, and this served as a guide to remind me of what was going on.

Basically I jotted a word or two about each day: if we went to the garden or had a bath, and such great events as the visit of a kitten to our room and the time Hamid got the car stuck taking us to the garden. I also noted when I received mail, which was very infrequently.

The students had begun to tell us all kinds of stories about the mail: The CIA had stopped it. The U. S. government was stopping it to drive us crazy. The post office was being reorganized. The truth of the matter was, the students couldn't possibly read and censor all the stuff that was coming to us, and they simply didn't care. If they gave us one card every two weeks, why should we need anything else?

I missed mail from my family so much! One way I tried to deal with the problem was to offer it to God as a sacrifice. But I soon realized just how far short I fell of making that sacrifice real. I was running one night when I found myself thinking I would rather have mail than *anything* else—almost more than knowing God Himself! I sat down to ponder this new realization. It was a sharp blow, but how beautiful to know I could be forgiven for it. I had a long, long way to go in my spiritual journey. I hoped my sacrifices of the other things that felt good, like anger, resentment and rebelliousness would fare better.

Another new development: Hamid arrived to announce that we should keep track of our meals, for they were now being prepared by the students. The cook had left! (We assumed the late-night gunfire had been too much for him.)

Confident that I could handle the cooking chores for 5 or 55 (I'd never been able to plan a dinner party for fewer than 15 and had prepared for up to 250!), I promptly volunteered once more to help in the kitchen.

"No, no, you are our guest," came the stock protest.

The first few days were not too bad. The students tried to fry shrimp, and it was a bit salty. But the situation deteriorated rapidly.

Lunch came later and later, and a few times not at all. It was Iranian food, not bad itself, but horridly prepared.

I had always liked Iranian food. Iranians have some of the best rice in the world. When well prepared, it has a crispy crunchy crust called *tadick*, which is splendid. The *horeshts* or stew-like toppings that are served with the rice can be very good, filled with all sorts of goodies from stewed fruits, nuts, and raisins to lovely savory combinations of greens and french fried potatoes.

To supplement these vegetable combinations, they continuously nibble raisins and all sorts of lovely fresh fruits: apricots, plums, apples, oranges, and pomegranates as well as nuts and sunflower and melon seeds.

Needless to say, we now were given none of these, and we missed them sorely. On occasions we were given nuts or seeds, but only as a treat.

Supper was "American" food, which to the students meant heating up whatever was in a can: tuna fish, sardines, or kidney beans. Thank goodness for the tasty bread and butter at breakfast, and our habit of hoarding whatever came our way. If cheese wasn't available, I would take jam, eat some, and give the rest to Ann to store in our extra supplies. We did complain when food failed to come. Finally, whoever was responsible for our food started sending out for

150

ice cream to make us feel better, and occasionally when meals were forgotten they sent for hamburgers. We were so hungry, even foreign interpretations of the all-American meal tasted good.

Things finally got so bad that Ann kept a detailed diary of everything served. We knew only too well how bad off we were. We started taking Geritol. The students had found a supply, kindly bringing it around about once a month and giving us each a single capsule. After repeated requests, we finally got our own bottles of Geritol and multiple vitamins, and we took one each daily.

Life was looking pretty bleak indeed, with such a poor diet. One morning during my quiet time, I began to write some of my questions and thoughts in what I came to call a "spiritual diary." I never intended it to be more than a memory aid for myself, but the exercise proved to be an encouragement during those long, monotonous days.

> June 12—Renewed sacrifice of grumbling and rebellion, resentment—pray it will work as letter sac. [sacrifice] didn't! I still can feel the sting of that blow when I put my letter god above my Saviour. *O, Lord how merciful You are to assure me I am forgiven that.* Such a full day—realization that this isolated extremity being prayed for by the Body of the Believers can pray from its weakness for those who are really hurting! I do have the *Word*—in three versions and the hymnal—Praise be to Thee, O Beloved Saviour!
>
> Start a spiritual diary—May it help me grow! The Word came during meditation, and I think I heard the still small voice say that my sacrifices were acceptable. How lovely to be reassured. *Thanks be to God for lessons received. Amen.*

That same day I wrote a poem:

> *No matter when I come to Him*
> *He has the time for me*
> *He stops and cares and listens*
> *Whatever the hour be—*

151

I come to Him in the morning
To thank Him for the day
And stay for several hours
To listen, watch and pray.

I come again at evening
When the day is done
And once again He listens
To all my pleas—each one.

He never seems too hurried
For me and all my needs
But gives me full attention
And ne'er from me recedes.

Why can't I do the same
To those around me still
Why can't I find the time
When they their hearts unfill.

O grant me, Lord, the courage
To work for Thee this way
To listen, really listen
To what my neighbors say.

To listen and to come
With them to Thee in prayer
For, Lord, I know You'll listen
We'll ever find You there.

And Lord, give me the Grace
To listen, know, and heed
When You would speak to me
To answer someone's need.

Lord, I love Thy presence
I love to talk to Thee
Help me, O Lord, to listen
When You would speak to me.

My equanimity was restored—for a while. We survived lunch and settled in to our afternoon reading. At about 5:00,

152

gunfire erupted near the compound, and the disturbance continued unabated for several hours and sounded as if it was coming nearer and nearer. No one would tell us what was happening, and Ann and I grew more and more apprehensive. We were almost angry when finally Hamid came to assure us it had nothing to do with us. Supposedly a group of protesters was meeting at the nearby athletic stadium, and Khomeini loyalists wanted to break up the meeting. So they called in the guns to keep the peace.

We were so keyed up we got our "get away bags" ready to grab. We also tried to arrange a hiding place. Simply put, we were terrified.

> June 13—A Friday and quiet. No march-bys [demonstrations] after Friday prayers. It was the kind of day that was filled with thoughts of praise! I would have loved to have spent the whole day just thinking, so welcome after yesterday afternoon's gunfire for hours.
>
> I have felt from the beginning that God is taking care of me. I must simply be patient and I will leave here to do His will. One night when I was particularly despondent God led me to read verses 17 and 18 of Psalm 118: "I shall not die, but live, and declare the works of the LORD. The LORD hath chastened me sore: but he hath not given me over unto death." This beautiful promise affirmed what I had felt from the beginning—that I would be free again one day. It was only later that I began to prepare myself more fully to "declare the works of the Lord." This verse, of course, came flooding back during the terrifying hours and was really a source of comfort. God cares—He wants me to come out of this alive and declaring His works!
>
> June 14—Tonight while I was running I came to a real understanding of what the wife of the Bishop of the Lutheran Church in Romania meant when she asked me to pray for the Lutheran Church in Romania. I had asked her in one of our talks if there was anything our churches outside the [Communist] Bloc could do for them and was surprised when she said, "Our needs are well met, but ask everyone to pray for us." I understood what she meant when I remembered I had written to Annie, "Thank ev-

153

eryone for their prayers; it is the thing that supports us daily!" Praise be to God this should help me reassess my prayer life, the work God has given me to do here and now.

As I wrote more and more, I began to see more clearly the ups and downs of this day-to-day battle for stability.

June 17—There must be a lesson in today—somewhere! The food situation is getting worse—Argue before a small amount of cheese was brought for breakfast. Lunch was late and was warmed-up tuna. Period. Supper was even later—warmed-up kidney beans and the saving thing, lovely bing cherries! No tea most of the day. Ann was hauled off for questions at 11:30 P.M. All so senseless— what am I to learn? I can still be thankful for a cool breeze tonight, and for the Word. I'd better dig deep. I have a longing for some devotional guides. Dorothy's latest have not arrived. The mail is really fouled up! Thank goodness for books and meditation. Somewhere in this wasteland must be something. I'll pray for understanding and patience! *Lord, thank You for staying with me!*

June 19—For many years I've wondered about the "personal knowledge of Jesus as Lord and Saviour." Because I was brought up in the Church, I knew and felt that I was a child of God. I held fast to the promise of Eternal Life and knew that I would, dying in the Faith that Jesus had died for my sins, awaken in Heaven. But I had always wondered about this "personal" knowledge. My wonder increased as I read and studied about the Holy Spirit [earlier] during my "hostageship." Much that I had read made me believe that there might be a "personal" knowledge that I was missing!

I felt very close to the Father—that was easy, for after all, I had wonderful parents, people who had brought me to God in baptism, taught me the difference between right and wrong, and who had the marvelous ability to let us go—make our own mistakes or decisions, but who

154

were there to help us. I understood a beautiful Father-Child relationship and turned eagerly to Our Father.

The evidence of the work of the Holy Spirit during these months had been overwhelming—things remembered, peace, joy and love, my special spiritual communion—but Jesus, my Lord and Saviour—elusive. I couldn't "relate" to Him. I had prayed for an open heart so that I might understand and walk more closely with Him. But I could not identify Him—friend, brother, teacher—nothing seemed to be it. Then while reading the chapter called "Jesus" in Carlo Caretto's book *In Search of the Beyond*, my mind was caught on the following words "It is a question of God *as He is,* not as He may appear to us or as we may imagine Him."

My mind was released, and I was in the presence of my Saviour. I, too, had a personal knowledge of my Saviour. I was surrounded by His presence. I can't describe it. Like many others—I knew it was He. I felt His love and had a sense of light—and the sum total was that there was nothing else outside of Him. This lasted only briefly, but the memory is warm, and colored everything that followed. I hope I am privileged to experience this again and again—but if not, I *know* it and that is what is important.

God, keep my heart and soul ever open to receive You as You are, not as I imagine You to be. Amen.

Just when I thought we could take no more warmed up sardines, our overseer guard changed. The new guard's name was Ahkbar, and one night late in June, he arrived with a sheepish request. "Hahnum Koob, you can cook, can't you?"

"Can I cook?!"

I slipped on my blindfold instantly and was led off down the hall. Down the steps—count them off: eight, then fourteen, and then to the left—to the chancellery kitchenette.

There was Ahkbar, desperately trying to make an edible meal out of some two-year-old hamburgers. They were like pieces of leather, freezer burned and swimming in a frying pan filled with oil. I took the situation in at a glance, closed my eyes and nose to the dirt, clutter, and grease and asked, "How many are we cooking for?"

I was told four, plus Ann and myself.

"I don't think there is enough food here for four men," I ventured, and Ahkbar, totally defeated, said I could cook anything in the kitchen.

I set about taking stock. The stove had only two burners, but there was a hot plate on a table. And yes, the oven worked.

The grease went from the skillet, more hamburgers were pulled from the freezer, and miracle of miracles, there was a gold mine of frozen, thawed, refrozen (to the tenth power, I'm sure) vegetables. I set pots to boiling. In the midst of these preparations, who should show up but my roomie, Ann, who announced that although she couldn't cook much she was great with the dishpan. A cook should have it so good!

The menu was slim beyond hamburgers and soggy vegetables that evening, but there was plenty of it, along with catsup (available in a number 10 can) and pickles, too. We also managed a simple dessert of canned fruit. It was wonderful! We were out of our room, doing something creative, serving some of our fellow hostages, and having some control over our calorie and nutrition intake.

Later that night Ann and I wondered aloud if such an opportunity would ever happen again. It did! Inside of a week, we had been named the cooks for our little enclave. An entire new batch of problems came with this task, of course, but the challenge gave a fresh focus to our days. Hesitantly, our guards showed up with a copy of the *Tehran-American Women's Club Cookbook*. It not only had recipes that were adapted to Iran but also included an English-Farsi vocabulary in the back. It was full of helpful items, like how to use yogurt in place of sour milk.

We started by looking for recipes that called for the items we had on hand. Early on, we had dozens of eggs, and many of them were cracked and needed to be used. We came

156

up with an egg Florentine recipe: eggs poached in a rich cheese sauce, served on English muffins (from the freezer) and spinach. All we needed was grated cheese on top. No grater. We called on our Yankee ingenuity to make one. Looking about the kitchen, we found a small tin can and a nail. With the nail we punched holes in the bottom of a tuna tin and made our own grater. Not the most efficient thing in the world, but it worked. The eggs Florentine were outstanding. The plates came back empty.

The kitchen itself was a nightmare. The kids knew we had a thing about cleanliness, so they had done their best to make things right. But they apparently had never heard of cleanser and elbow grease. Full plastic garbage bags were everywhere. More plastic bags had been spread over dirty work surfaces, and underneath them were whole cities of little creeping, crawling things.

I hated to clean up, but I hated working in a dirty kitchen far more. In about a week we felt secure enough in our new roles to begin a thorough scrubdown. My first attempt was with the stove. Eight months of encrustation responded reasonably well to hot water and soap, and ultimately a scouring powder. A cat appeared to watch the proceedings, and although we were initially afraid of rabies, she soon endeared herself to our hearts, especially when she appeared with a brand new kitten. The students had little use for animals, so we allowed her to stay with us. She watched quietly as Ann tackled the dishes, and day by day the plastic bags were removed, and the accumulated grime was cleaned away. We eventually got the countertop and tables cleaned, the floor mopped, and the cupboard clean.

The piled-up garbage was a continual problem, however. Eventually it got so bad again that we talked to one of the medical students and pointed out that the situation was a health hazard to them as well as to us. Reluctantly, some new plastic garbage bags were brought. We cleaned out the old, happily relined the trash cans, and then for days stumbled over the bags we had tied up and the students had moved into the hallway. "Well," mumbled Ann, "at least *they're* looking at them now."

To protect certain kitchen items we used everyday, we deliberately chose not to clean the cupboard area under the sink. We figured, rightly as it turned out, that the students would not want to use items from a dirty location if clean things were available. Here we stored our most prized possession, a Skippy peanut butter jar with measuring cup markings on the side.

I was glad I'd lived in the Third World before and so was acquainted with "living Bisquick." We threw some items out and froze the grains and flours to kill the moving creatures, then sifted them out. If I had had any idea we all had protein deficiencies, perhaps I wouldn't have sifted quite so assiduously!

Salvaging the hamburgers that had gotten us to the kitchen in the first place proved a futile task. We tried a dozen different methods of cooking them the first few days, including shredding and pounding them into regular ground beef, but they always tasted the same: dreadful! As a last resort we marinated them overnight, then cooked them slowly in the oven, stuffed with cheese, tomato, and onion and buried in a barbecue sauce. But still they were no good.

The students were proud of our cooking, though, and often asked if we needed anything. Trying to communicate that we needed a spoon or a sieve sometimes produced funny results, but persistence paid off; and eventually we were able to accumulate an odd but rudimentary collection of cooking utensils.

The students were doing some of their own cooking, too, and they liked to "borrow" our equipment—can openers, paring knives, tea kettles. (There was no hot water in the kitchen, so tea kettles were in constant use.) Each evening in the kitchen usually began by sending the sister out to look for the serving dishes we had used the night before, digging leftovers out of the refrigerator in the upstairs hall, and scouring the building to find the saucepans.

158

All our hard work drew an unexpected reward. One night when the empty trays came back to the kitchen, we discovered a tiny note signed, "The Boys in the Back Room." We knew we were cooking for four other hostages, but we had never seen them and had no idea who they were. Eagerly we started keeping a close watch on the wastebaskets, looking for clues. Ann ran into one of the men in the bathroom when the guards slipped up: sixty-five-year-old Bob Ode.* Then we found a package wrapping from "Hohman" in Germany. That had to be "Doc," an Army medic, and the guard let slip that "the Doctor" was a vegetarian. He also ate no sugar. Could we fix special meals for him? Bit by bit the puzzle was put together. The others we cooked for were Jerry Miele, a communications specialist, and Richard Queen, a consular official.**

Greatly encouraged, Ann and I began to plan our menus a week in advance, trying to work variety into the meals. We balanced lighter meals like tuna or chicken salad with heavier ones like pancakes. Pizza became a favorite and was easy to do. We used barbery bread (a very thin dough) as the crust, slathered it with a homemade pizza sauce (a combination of several recipes) and covered the whole thing with onions, green peppers, pre-cooked sausage, and cheese. Ann added anchovies to hers. It went under the broiler for five to seven minutes, and there it was, really good.

The notes kept coming. "Could you ask for more fresh fruits and vegetables? Could you explain to the guards that they have to go to the post office and pick up the mail?" (We nearly cried when we saw that, for we had our own running battle with the guards trying to get our mail!) "Could you make chocolate chip cookies, peanut butter cookies, pumpkin pie? Could you make *huevos rancheros* for the vege-

---

*A retired member of the foreign service who had been called to Tehran on a temporary assignment as special consular official.

**Queen was released on July 11 due to illness, eventually diagnosed as multiple sclerosis.

tarian? How about refried beans? The donuts were delicious. How about more popcorn?"

Eagerly we awaited each note. It was a bit of contact with other human beings, our colleagues. We took their suggestions seriously, and one by one we tried to give them what they wanted. We even found a recipe for flour tortillas!

The problem with requesting fresh fruits and vegetables was that they had to be purchased in the street market. Most of our food came from the embassy co-op, although we were not allowed to go personally to shop. Buying fresh food meant that one of the students had to make the effort to find money and to haggle in the marketplace. When he did, the food came in by the bushel, and we would have two weeks worth of tomatoes all needing to be eaten *now*!

Ann became very adept at sorting vegetables, determining which ones we could store a bit longer. But what do you do with a thirty-gallon garbage bag full of celery? Clean, cook, eat, dice, and try to be original. We found out that celery braised with rosemary makes a very good addition to a "Greek" salad plate. I didn't know of any Greeks who would agree, but with cold beets, black olives, a bit of greens, the cold braised celery, and a generous serving of white cheese, our "Greek salad" with garlic breadsticks made from leftover barbery was spectacular.

The Fourth of July was coming. Ann and I were determined to do something special, so we decided to bake a chocolate cake. But we had no idea how to decorate it. Ann was feeling a bit down, so before we went to bed on July 3, I reached in my drawer and pulled out a firecracker. I had covered a toilet paper tube with a piece of red paper cut from an envelope. A scrap of yarn held a bit of silver tinsel in place as a fuse. "Happy 4th of July" was written on a bit of blue and white paper cut from the inside of another envelope, and was taped rakishly across the side of the firecracker.

Ann grinned when she saw it, and we set out to make tiny ones from the scraps. When kitchen duty came that day, we shoved them in the toothpaste tube caps taken from our

160

supplies and carried them off to the kitchen to perch in the frosting. With fried chicken and potato salad, we had a real picnic dinner. That night as we cleaned up our dishes in the bathroom we were delighted to see three little firecrackers marching in a row behind the wastebasket.*

With the diversion of cooking the evening meal, the focus of my diary seemed to deepen more and more on thoughts of Christ.

> July 10—This morning as I was praying I was going to use the phrase "I approach Thy Throne, O Lord . . ." and realized I don't have to approach the throne at all if Christ abides in me, and I in Him. I'm at the throne. O Lord, what a fantastic thought! *At the throne.* And then tonight while I was running, I realized a little bit more that that was part of that verse in Luke—chapter 17: "The Kingdom of God is within you." At the throne! Christ in me, I in Him! Would that this clay pot would pour forth only His love and reflect only His grace and glory!
>
> *Lord help me to remember always I'm at the throne and to act like it!*
>
> July 11—A letter from Dr. Preus** today! How welcome—and Romans 8! I had just spent two bedtime devotions reading it, and I never fail to thrill to the clanging resonance of the closing words (which I love to hear read from the King James version).
>
> "For I am persuaded, that neither death, nor life, nor angels, nor principalities, nor powers, nor things present, nor things to come, nor height, nor depth, nor any other creature, shall be able to separate us from the love of God, which is in Christ Jesus our Lord." How often I've let those words just flow over me, and what peace and wonder each time I read them!

---

*We didn't realize then that this may have been an attempt by the men to tell us that Richard Queen was either no longer with them or unable to eat. After Queen was sent home, not wanting us to know, the students told us to cook for three others because one of the men wanted "only Iranian food."

**The president of the American Lutheran Church.

And Romans 8, verse 6: ". . . but the mind controlled by the Spirit is life and peace." What a beautiful promise. *Holy Spirit, take my mind and help it always to seek to follow my Lord's will. As with cards and letters from so many people, how humble I feel that so much effort should be expended in prayer—and how grateful I am for that support! O Lord, help me ever to pray for others! Amen.*

July 12—A swift response to prayer! I had asked to be taught to love the students. I like many of them as individuals, but love them?—my captors? Yet we are told so clearly we must—and this is further complicated by their denial of Christ as the Son of God in their "Islamness." This morning in desperation, I asked *how*. And at the close of my devotions a lovely answer was waiting for me in *In Search of the Beyond*. Chapter 16, "Blessed Are the Merciful." To paraphrase—Accept what they have done. Do not appeal to reason or justice but to the path of love. Act to them in love. Jesus overrode justice with love when He died for us.

Maybe it's making cookies, maybe it's just being pleasant, but in all things it calls for acts of love! Do not deny the truth of the situation, but go beyond it in love. *Now, Lord, show me how I do this! May my heart be open to Thy Spirit's promptings! Amen.*

Despite my deepening awareness of activity in the heavens, the earthly summer dragged on and on. My sacrifices and feelings kept being tested.

Some of our guards were very curious about our activities in the kitchen, and they offered gratuitous advice in abundance: "Don't run the water. That is wasteful." "You should give the leftover food to the animals." That we could stand, but it did bother us when they would literally stick their noses into whatever it was we were cooking. I have never seen people who could get their noses quite so deep into a cooking pot as the sisters.

Because Ahkbar liked sweets, he continually stressed to us how important it was to make dessert. So we turned out cookies, cakes, donuts, pies, brownies, and other delights. But the guards had insatiable sweet tooths, and often we would return to the kitchen to find all the jam and baked goods completely decimated. We tried to keep honey on hand for Doc Hohman; it and chocolate syrup and cocoa were particularly choice items. The challenge to hide and hoard food fluctuated between being a game and a real irritation.

But there were small rewards, too. I'm sure one family in Tehran today eats garlic sticks because of what their daughter learned in our kitchen. Ann and I tore leftover bread into crouton or breadstick-size pieces, froze it, and then made fresh garlic croutons or sticks as our menus called for it. One guard named Sheba watched us do this one night, and the next day reported that her family thought it was an excellent way to use leftover bread.

It was agreed: Going to the kitchen was excellent for Ann and me. Cooking was good therapy, and more importantly than anything else, we learned that service is a good antidote for the blues.

Shah dies; Iranians rejoice/
Hostage crisis unchanged,
Tehran leaders say
Des Moines Register
July 28, 1980

12

JULY–OCTOBER, 1980

It was full summer: hot, dry, and very quiet. But the torpor induced by the heat was shattered temporarily when we learned some of the details of the attempted rescue. We first learned that it had happened on July 17 when a letter from a school child slipped by the censor. She wrote that she was sorry the rescue attempt had failed, and she hoped they would try again. We didn't share that hope. We thought a rescue attempt would end up a blood bath. The students were determined to win, willing to die, and they had guns.

A couple of days later we were given back issues of news magazines, and we discovered eight men had been killed in that attempt to free us. I cannot describe how that affected me. I felt so small, humble, unimportant, and helpless. And we were frustrated, for we only knew bits and pieces of what had occurred. We couldn't understand the whole incident, but we did pray for the men's families. That we could do.

The long, hot days dragged on. Without my diary I could have easily drifted into sleepwalking day after day.

July 27—A quiet Sunday that almost made me feel weary. I am tired—not physically, but mentally and morale-wise. A low day, but so weary of *not* having proper church,

164

of writing family letters that say nothing (and probably aren't even posted! Lying on the hall table!) but which must be written. Thank goodness the one thing that doesn't tire or weary me is coming to God in prayer and meditation—there is always another of His promises for me to think about—and today I must think about Matthew 11:28 "Come unto me, all of you who are tired of carrying heavy loads, and I will give you rest!"

O Lord, how often You have given me rest during these past months. Once again I follow Peter's advice and cast all of my cares on You so that I can rest, knowing You will give me strength to shoulder this burden again and again and again. "Take my hand, dear Father, and lead Thou me." On Thy strong Name I lean. Amen.

July 29—Received mail (from February and July!) today from the family. It was also confirmed that the letters we have been writing have not been sent! Things are supposed to have changed! We still wait for word that our families are receiving mail! But even though we feel burdened by length of confinement and what may lie ahead, tonight there is deep comfort in the strength of the Lord.

How marvelous are Thy ways, O Lord. Thank You for making our load bearable. O Lord, if You bore it all on Calvary, why can't we let You carry it in how we react to these loads. I'm not sure what I'm trying to say, but I simply rest in Your strength and say thank You for what You have given me! Amen.

August 13—A question that has bothered me for sometime is: If Christ bore all our sins to the Cross and died on the Cross for us, why do we also have to bear the cross for a second time?

Last night as I was thinking about this in the wee hours, I realized that Christ died for us after bearing the cross, but that even as Simon of Cyrene physically bore Christ's cross on the road to Golgotha, he did not die. Bearing the cross is the least part of Good Friday. The death on the cross was the real work. That has been done for us. Oh, we may die to the world, but that is to come alive in eternity with our Lord.

165

Even as Simon was given a unique opportunity to know the Lord when he carried that crucifixion cross, so we come to know our Christ when we bear our crosses. No wonder when it is heaviest it seems to be lightened by our Saviour. He knows all about cross-bearing and beyond. *Thank You, Lord, for my cross. Amen.*

August 14—Another day, another question. Why do we seem to have to learn the same lessons over and over? Seems like when we learned our "times" tables we didn't forget them. Why can't we learn lessons of temper control, humility, and love once? Or is it that we know the lesson and just don't use it? Those "times" tables don't do us much good if we don't use them, even if we know them perfectly. Maybe we know the lesson and that's why it seems we're "learning" it again when we recognize our failure to use it. For if we didn't know it, how could we know we hadn't used it?

Thank You, Lord, for having taught us the lessons well enough that we hurt when we forget to put them to work. Amen.

September 14—I feel like I'm ready to fall apart—only tears and nerves holding me together. Lies, lies, and more lies from the students, and then when I think I can take no more I hear the voice of the Shepherd. "I am the good shepherd; I know my sheep and my sheep know me—just as the Father knows me and I know the Father—and I lay down my life for the sheep." If He laid down His life for me, He gives me life, and the healing streams of living waters pours through me and I recover.

How powerful, how beautiful are Thy ways, O Lord. Thank You for streams of living waters and healing. Amen.

The summer had passed, a quiet hiatus in our bizarre, isolated little world. Some days included unexpected pleasures. At one point we received a packet of needlework, accompanied by a note signed "Meg." We had been given a packet of toiletries earlier from the same person. With a little detective work, I deduced our benefactor was the wife of Sir John Graham, the British ambassador to Iran. In the note, she mentioned having heard from the Lows; he was the United States ambassador to Zambia while I was there. Knowing that Ambassadors Low and Graham had worked together in southern Africa, and that Lady Graham's name was Margaret, we figured out the source of our surprises.

Then, abruptly, our calm little world changed again. On the afternoon of September 22, there were more comings and goings than usual in the chancellery. What was up? People were moving up and down the central staircase, rapidly.

When we went blindfolded to the kitchen to prepare our evening meal, we had to stand to the side of the hall more than once to let people pass. The footsteps were different from the light rapid steps of the students. All sorts of people were talking to each other in Farsi, and the voices were voices we had not heard before.

After being rushed through dinner preparation and sending plates up to the men, the sister tied our blindfolds tightly back in place, and we grabbed our own dinner trays. When we returned to our room, a brother named Moiseni was busy covering one of our two windows with black garbage bags. The other window, which had an air conditioner in it, was heavily draped with blankets.

"What is happening?" we asked.

"There is a blackout, just for tonight," he answered.

We couldn't figure out what was going on. The sister who had been with us in the kitchen had been almost frantic, insisting we hurry our cooking and leave. Now Moiseni was putting up these black garbage bags. I looked at Ann, and she looked at me. We assisted Moiseni as best we could, handing up the tape to him. He and the sister finally finished and left the room.

"What do you think?" asked Ann. "Should we get our get-away bags ready?" They had been packed for months.

"That's a good idea. I think we'd better go through them again." We double-checked everything and packed our last-

167

minute toiletries. We had hoped once before that perhaps in the confusion we could get away. We wanted those bags ready.

The tension in the air increased, and we prayed about it in our evening devotions, asking the Lord to give us wisdom to act knowledgeably and wisely should anything happen. We waited for something, anything. Nothing happened. Finally we decided to spend the evening in our usual fashion: reading, exercising, and eventually going to bed.

The next day was no different. The blackout continued. We were allowed to open the drapes over the air conditioner to let daylight in, but that was small comfort. How awful it seemed sitting in that small room, looking up where we once had been able to see sky and treetops and seeing nothing but large black plastic bags. We had become good friends with the treetops, the sky, and the moon, and we missed them.

The kids refused to say anything about what was going on. "Can we take the blackout thing off the window?" we persisted.

"It's not your concern . . . nothing you need worry about," they answered evasively. "It'll go away. Don't worry about it."

What was to be only for one night continued into another day. At 10:30 the next evening, the sister came into the room and announced, "You must turn off the lights. You may have a candle."

We did our sit-ups and pushups in the dark and tried to plan menus by the lights in the corridor. Ann took the cookbook and slipped it under the edge of the door, but she could read only two lines of print from the light that came in. Finally we gave up and turned in.

The blackout was into its fourth night when we heard airplanes overhead and gunfire around the embassy. It sounded like anti-aircraft gunfire—KA-BOOM! KA-BOOM! This was definitely not the familiar gunshots that we were used to from the students' G-3s going off. Still no clue as to what was happening.

168

We were taken to the garden the next day for exercise. I long ago had lost my shoes, and now wore only plastic flip-flops, so I was walking rather than jogging in the familiar little walled-in courtyard. Something struck me about the residence, and I turned to Ann, who was running. "Ann, the next time you go by the window, look inside. It's empty." The residence was deserted! One more question to try to answer.

We tried again to question the sisters, with little cooperation on their part. However, after a few more days, one of the students did tell us Iran and Iraq were "at odds." "Just as I thought," Ann, who was very astute politically, said to me later. "If the invader had been the United States, we would be treated differently. And if it were the Soviet Union, there would be a lot more shouting in the streets." But we still had no word on what was actually happening.

Two days later, heavy gunfire erupted by the kitchen window as we attempted to serve up dinner by candlelight. The sisters were absolutely terrified, and after a few minutes of trying to finish dishing out the meal under the table, the girls rushed us out of the kitchen back to our room. The gunfire went on for quite some time.

We began to hear air raid drills now throughout the day: the long wail of the siren and instructions in Farsi, followed very often by military music. After persistent questioning, we were assured by the brothers these were "practice air raid drills," and we need not worry about them. The nation needed everyone to be alert in case there should be an air attack. "It doesn't concern you. It's none of your affair."

"What do you mean, 'It's none of your affair'?" I shot back. "If there are air raids and bombs dropping, it certainly is our affair!"

The firing and the sirens were coming all too regularly, and some days we could see the flames as the shells exploded in the air. How much did our families know? Were they worried about us? To add to our tension, the students stood in the compound courtyard blasting into the air with their G-3s during the air raids. "You have to understand," one of the brothers explained mildly, "these kids have been carrying guns for a long time without any excuse to use them."

"Some way, somehow the Lord will walk us away from this," I wrote in my diary. "Dear Lord, keep me cool and calm, ready to listen to Thy word and to follow Thee instantly without hesitation."

One of the students stopped by to tell us how he had had a nervous breakdown over the whole ordeal of taking care of us. We couldn't believe it! He insisted the responsibility of seeing to our needs was so great it had brought him to the verge of collapse. We should sympathize with him, we were told, and understand what our being there was doing to him.

In the midst of all of this, Ann and I tried to retain our sense of humor. One particular day brought a surprising lift of morale. It was the middle of the day, and the sirens were going full blast. We heard the same old announcements in Farsi, the second siren, and then I couldn't believe my ears. There was no mistaking the distinctive tune of John Philip Sousa's "Stars and Stripes Forever." I wanted to stand up and cheer, but Ann and I just looked at each other and grinned. I wondered if this was somebody's Freudian slip, wishing they had better relations with the United States so they could seek our help in the current crisis.

October came, and with it, my birthday. Ann worked hard to make it special, and we had a lovely day in spite of the blackouts, "air raid drills," and our restricted residency in the chancellery. She wrote me some poems for birthday cards she designed, and with the help of the students she managed to find me a new shirt. She also insisted that I make a burnt sugar cake. She made ice cream and fudge sauce. (After our self-imposed dieting, I'm surprised we both weren't sick.) And glory of glories, we finally got some fresh vegetables and some apples. Oh, did they taste good!

The day after my birthday, Tiger Lily stopped in to chat. We were seeing her a little more regularly now. She came to announce that Iraq had stooped to very low tactics. The Iraqis were dropping paper table napkins contaminated with something that would cause cancer in the city. According to her, these were beautiful floral napkins that people could not resist. But as a result of handling them, they would get cancer.

It seemed incredible to us that Tiger Lily's intelligence would allow her to swallow such blatant propaganda. But at least her tirade gave us a clue to the circumstances.

Through all of this, Ann and I held our regular church services each Sunday. Our prayers became more specific. We asked that Iraq and Iran would find a way to solve their differences, and we asked for strength and wisdom to know how to act in whatever situation might come along.

The electricity began to go off for two hours each day. Sometimes it was early morning, sometimes early afternoon and, occasionally, when we wanted to cook. Those times we opted to make a cold salad. We concluded that since the electricity failure seemed to be very systematic, all sections of the city were being blacked out to conserve electricity. This had also been done during the revolution.

Toward the end of the month, Akhbar, one of the more trustworthy students, leaked to us the news that negotiations were underway and that within ten days we would be going home. We were stunned. Could we trust this piece of information? Was it a ploy? We dared not get our hopes up. Incongruously, in the height of all this tension we received a postcard from one of our State Department colleagues telling us we didn't have to pay income taxes! We were surprised at the news and grateful, but it seemed totally immaterial at this point.

Then, on October 30, we heard noises in the night, noises we had come to associate with moving. But the brothers never came for us. "Are the men going home?" we asked each other. We committed them to the Lord's care. Anything could be happening.

Once more, we had the desolate feeling we had been left behind. It was eerie knowing that Ann and I were probably the only two Americans in the chancellery, although the girls

171

tried very hard to make us believe the men were still there. When we asked to go to the toilet, they pretended to check to see if somebody was in the bathroom, or they said they would have to ask the brothers. But we knew the brothers were not in the building, either. Moiseni, who was left behind as supervisor, finally blew the girls' cover when he told us we should prepare food only for ourselves. For us, it was the ultimate desolation. The fun went out of the cooking.

When would this game be over?

13

NOVEMBER, 1980

With the men gone, the sisters grew nervous and trigger happy. Ann and I had become very good at positioning ourselves so that when the sisters opened the door, one of us could surreptitiously look out over her shoulder. The girls in the hall made a grab for their guns as soon as the door opened. None of them had been trained in weaponry, which made them all the more prone to use guns in case something happened. The situation put Ann and me on edge.

Moiseni was little comfort. After two days of the quiet, he appeared in the kitchen. I broke down and asked, "Moiseni, can you tell us, have the men gone home?" We really hoped they had, even if it meant we had been left.

He smiled, slowly, in his inscrutable way. "I'm sorry, Hahnum Koob, I can't tell you where they've gone."

Ann and I exchanged glances and silently set about finishing dinner preparations for the two of us.

"Days of putting everything back in the hands of God," I wrote in my diary. "How quickly one falls into the trap of 'trusting in princes,' when everything can and does then fall apart. So blessed be the Lord who unchanging waits once more for me to say, 'As You will, Lord. I'm in Your hands. Open my heart to hear Your will.'"

173

I had been using my mattress and blankets as a daytime sofa, but now the walls were too cold to lean against. I asked if I could have a chair. After all, the chancellery was deserted. For once, with no questions or pretense, a fine leather easy chair appeared in the room.

Nights, Ann and I sat with our heads underneath the coffee table, reading by the light of a lamp covered with two blankets so no light would show outside.

We had reached the end of a week and it was time to plan another week's food. "Ann, what shall we fix?"

"I don't know," she sighed. "I don't really care. But we can't let ourselves mope around. Let's plan some menus."

We sat down, she with her feet tucked up under her, me curled up in my newly acquired chair, and talked half-heartedly about cooking. We had planned to have lamb on the anniversary of the take-over—a new culinary challenge for both of us.

"Guess we'll go ahead and cook it. We'll need to freeze some of the other stuff we've already prepared."

"No need to do much baking anymore, either."

We really missed the boys in the back room, although we had never talked to them. The building was *so very quiet.*

The evening of November 12, the girls came tapping at the door. "Get your things ready. You're going to be moved."

"Where are we going?" I asked.

"I can't tell you. Just get ready."

Our get-away bags were as ready as ever, but we had other things we wanted to take along. We had acquired a shelf of cookbooks. "Will we be cooking?" I asked.

"I don't know," said a sister.

"Well, we should take some of our cookbooks with us. Will you move them for us?"

"We'll see," was the only answer I could get. One sister did come back to tell us there would be only male guards at our next stop.

So we started packing. We used our pillowcases and some plastic bags we had been given at Eastertime. Our

174

vitamin pills, toothpaste, and toiletries went into one bag; games and special books into a box; plants, colored paper, and materials for special decorations went into another bag. Embroidery floss, yarn for needlework: so trivial but so important in helping to pass the time. Our books—it had taken us so long to acquire them, and we didn't know when we'd see the library again. We sorted and made a selection.

We made our bundles as compact as we possibly could, but we still knew we'd lose some things. The Iranian men never liked to see us carrying things but usually "misplaced" whatever we let them handle.

I made sure *Imitation of Christ* was in with my toiletries bag and tucked my Bible and the hymnal under my arm. Ann's Bible was in her hand. By this time, our Bibles were interleaved with all sorts of things: pictures of our families, special letters, cards, and notes, and a letter for my mom and dad in case something happened to me. We tied them shut with string.

Finally, we said we were ready. Reluctantly we turned the bags over to the sisters and watched them leave the room.

This time, something new was added to the routine. Two of the girls came into the room and conducted a thorough body search. We had not had this kind of search since being taken hostage. The sister even made me take off my shoes so that she could feel the bottoms of my feet. I don't know what she thought I could hide. She came to my hip pocket, where I had tucked an extra copy of Ann's letter to her mom. I explained what it was. She took it out to the brother, and then she brought it back to me. I slipped it back into my pocket.

Our knives and forks—everything metal—was removed from our packs. I didn't know whether we'd find our twelve straight pins again or not. It was silly to be so concerned about straight pins, but it had taken us a year to accumulate these! We had carefully been hoarding them from wherever we could find them, in shirts brought us from the co-op and sometimes in the carpets as we'd cleaned the various rooms.

Finally our blindfolds were put on. We were told to dress warmly because we were going outside. Ann put her hand on my shoulder, and I offered my arm to the sister, as was our custom. Nope! Not this time. Tonight each of us had a guide, and we turned down the corridor to the *right*. We were leaving the chancellery.

Ann had a sudden thought. "Do take care of the cat and the kitten if we're not going to be where they can come. Will you bring them with us?" We had been feeding them in the kitchen.

"Don't worry, Elizabeth," reassured one of the sisters.* "We'll take care of them."

Down the end of the hall to the stairs. Twelve steps, turn, fourteen more steps to the bottom of the stairs. The cat and the kitten bounded past us. We were in the basement. Past the kitchen door, the two cats stopped. Ann and I were then led past the telephone room. A blast of cold air met us at the door. Down one step, up four steps, turn, up four more steps, stop. We could hear a motor running, and we climbed into a van, not a sedan. Vaguely I realized our cadre of sister guards was being replaced by brothers.

"Are you OK?" I managed to whisper to Ann as the vehicle lurched into motion. It was dusty and close in the van, and I could smell as much as hear that there were four or five brothers with us. *Just as long as they don't separate us,* I muttered to myself, trying to concentrate on where we were.

Obviously we were leaving the compound. We passed through the embassy gates onto the streets of the city. It was dark and quiet as the van picked up speed. We were going north.

Right, left, forward. I soon lost my bearings and couldn't

---

*Ann's name is Elizabeth Ann Swift. Her friends and family call her Ann. She was "Elizabeth" in Iran because the sound of her middle name was not acceptable in polite conversation.

figure out where we were. It seemed we drove forever at top speed. Finally we made a left hand turn and went down a rather steep incline. *Perhaps we're going into the basement of a building.* The van stopped; we got out. We could hear the marvelous sound of crickets and smell the clean night air. We were away from the city, and the night was so quiet, so very, very quiet.

Again, we were instructed to walk. Ann put her hand on my shoulder, and I held a scarf in my hand. The brother picked up the other end of the scarf and led us into a building. Up some steps, through a hallway, up more steps, down a long corridor, a couple of turns, and finally into a room.

"We're here. Take your blindfolds off!" he ordered. The room was very small: no windows, no way to look out. A sheet was hung across the door, but when it was held back, we could see. We were in a prison!

In the middle of the door was a very small window with iron bars. There were no beds, only two thin pallets on the floor and two straight-backed chairs. There was hardly room for us to turn around, but the cubicle was clean, scrupulously clean. The white sheets almost sparkled, and there were pillows. Blankets covered the floor. Someone had tried very hard to make our quarters as comfortable as possible.

Two brothers brought our bags in and set them down. Then in came our box of books; a bit later, our clothing. Ahkbar arrived with a couple of boxes of food. "Would you like some fruit?" he asked.

"That would be wonderful!"

"I have some mail for you," he said, handing us a small stack of letters.

"It's not opened!" I exclaimed.

"That's all right," he said. "You can go ahead and read it. I've got some magazines for you, too." And he held out some back issues of *Time* and *Newsweek*. We looked at them, amazed, and said thank you.

Ahkbar sat on a chair as I began to look through the mail. In a few minutes he reached into his pocket and

177

brought out another letter. Almost shyly he asked, "Do you have a special friend in Zambia?"

"Yes, I do."

Silenty he handed me a letter. I recognized the handwriting—Milton's—and started to cry.

He looked troubled and said, "Please don't do that."

"I haven't heard from this person in over a year. It's good to get his letter," I explained as I wiped away the tears. "Would you please be sure to mail the letters in the box back at the embassy?"

Ahkbar smiled. "You'll be home before they get there."

Ann and I both stopped what we were doing. "Don't say that, please, unless it's true!"

"I'm sure," he said mysteriously. "Things are happening."

Then he proceeded to give us our instructions. "If you need anything, knock on the door. There are no women guards here. The men will take care of you, but a woman will come here each day to check on you."

"Could we have some water?" I asked.

"Yes," he said.

He stuck his head out the door, and in a few minutes Ali arrived with a pitcher of water—the same little Ali who had been at the end of the hall the morning I had so determinedly gone to the bathroom without an escort. They were bidding us good night, so I had to speak quickly. "Excuse me, but I never had a chance to thank you for not using your gun when I went into the hall without my blindfold."

Half-startled, Ali only grinned and looked down at the floor as he left. I knew I had said the right thing.

Alone again, Ann and I looked around trying to decide where we would put our things. Then we remembered the magazines. We couldn't believe our eyes! There was a story about our colleagues, the Lijeks and the Staffords. They had gone to America. "What is the date on the magazine?' I asked.

"It's February," Ann said.

178

We sat down and read the whole magazine from cover to cover. What a gift! We were in jail, but now we knew the Staffords and Lijeks were home. And so were Bob Anders and Lee Schatz. What a terrific present! They had escaped under the cover of Canadian passports, with government help. "Am I glad I had Canadian friends before this happened," I said to Ann. "I always thought they were special, and now I know it."

We said a special "thank You" prayer that night for the safe escape of Kathy and Joe, Mark and Cora, Bob and Lee. Somebody else had gone home. "We'll get there, Ann," I said. "Just hang in there."

She grinned back. "I hope so, Kate . . . I hope so!"

The next morning tea came bright and early, accompanied by bread, cheese, and dates. Then one of the brothers knocked on the door. "Would you like to go outside for some fresh air?"

"Sure!" Ann said.

"Take your sweaters. It's cold out." He handed us two towels. "Here. Hold these over your eyes." No more blindfolds!

We held the towels over our eyes and marched through a couple of corridors to a room with a grill in the top instead of a roof. We could see nothing but the sky. The brother brought chairs for us to sit on, but we opted to walk around. Soon something attracted my attention. "Ann!" I said. "Some of the men have been here. Look!"

She came over to the corner where I was standing. There, scratched into the brick at eye level, was "Bill Daugherty, Paul Needham, April 28, 29, 30." "Right after the rescue attempt," I said. "I wonder if they are still here?"

Just then another brother knocked at the door. "Would you like some fruit?" he asked. He handed us oranges, some pomegranates, and a melon.

"They're beautiful!" I said. "Thank you so much."

"We hope your stay here will be as comfortable as possible," he said, politely, and left.

"Did you notice what he was wearing?" I asked Ann.

"Yes," she said. "I think it's a uniform of some sort."

"So do I. Do you suppose that means we're in the custody of the government instead of the students?" All kinds of ideas were running through our minds.

"I hope so. At least that way there'd be some control over what happens to us."

We were in the maximum security area of Evin prison, we learned later, for two days. Ahkbar brought more mail and a box from the co-op the second day, which yielded cans of chicken salad and plums, as well as a can opener, shampoo, soap, and other luxuries. He must have felt very badly about putting us in prison, for he soon returned. "We're going to move you. This is not good."

Once more we packed up our things, tied our blindfolds in place, and navigated the maze of corridors to another waiting van.

After traveling a very short distance, the van came to a halt on some gravel. We were led through a gate into a courtyard, warned not to talk, taken through a blanketed doorway, down a hall, and through another door into a room. "OK. Take your blindfolds off now." It was Ali speaking.

We were in a room slightly larger than our cubicle in the prison. "You have to be careful. It's a blackout," he warned. "Leave the blanket down."

So at least we had a window. That was good news. We put our packs down along the walls and spread our belongings out. The brothers brought us blankets and sheets, and we got ready to curl up for the night.

"I wonder where we are?" Ann said.

"I don't know, unless we can see something out that window."

"Well . . . let's look," she responded. We found a light switch, turned off the overhead light, and cautiously raised the blanket from the window. Nothing but total darkness. "I guess we'll have to wait till tomorrow to find out," Ann sighed. We said our prayers and tumbled into bed.

180

The next morning all sorts of bangings and noises in the corridor woke us. "Hey, I don't know where we are, but some of the guys are here," I said. "Listen."

"You're right. Who do you think that is next door? Can you hear anything?" Ann asked.

We put a glass to the wall. We could hear someone talking but couldn't distinguish the words. But the voice was definitely an American speaking English. Our spirits rose a bit.

"Look!" I said. "We can see out!" We raced over to the window. There was a metal shield that covered most of the frame, but we could peek around the edges. "There's a garden down there . . . with roses in it!"

"Look the other way!" Ann said. There were trees growing on the side of a mountain. "I wonder if we can get up in the window and see over the shield. Hey! Look down there. There are cars driving in and out."

"And smell that," I said. "It smells like fresh baked bread."

We were to learn a lot about this place in the next few days, though we stayed in our room. From what we could gather, this had been offices or quarters for those who were working at the prison. We were permitted to use two bathrooms; one with a shower. We soon discovered we were sharing these with the American men. There were razors on the shelf, and more than once we could hear their heavy footsteps in the corridor. Miracle of miracles, we could look out into the courtyard through tiny holes that someone had scratched in the paint on the bathroom windows. We resisted the impulse to enlarge those holes so they would escape notice from the guards.

I came back from my first trip to the toilet full of excitement. "Ann! Colonel Schaefer* was exercising in the courtyard! But I didn't recognize the other guys with him."

---

*Air Force Col. Thomas E. Schaefer, the defense and air attaché at the embassy.

Each time we went to use one of the toilets, we looked out the window and listened carefully to see if we could figure out who was exercising. We definitely identified Colonel Scott.* And then one day, when we were sunning in the courtyard, Ann murmured, "Don't look now, but check the bathroom window." Looking out the unpainted top half of the window was Al Golacinski,** and he was waving like crazy. We couldn't even let him know we'd seen him; the guard was sitting right there talking to us. But to know these men were all right brought us great joy and relief.

Now that we were in a more informal arrangement, the brothers came in and asked if we could help again with the cooking. The "kitchen" was a storeroom connected to our room by a small corridor walled off from the main hallway. A gas hot plate was brought in, and Ann and I set about extending whatever dinner was brought over from the prison with more American-type fare.

We began using our window as a refrigerator, hoarding away portions of the regular meals and then rearranging the food to suit ourselves. Leftover rice was turned into rice pudding. Because butter and cheese did not come on a regular basis, we saved extra to use on days it was scarce. Yogurt with a bit of cinnamon could do wonders for even the most tasteless canned fruit.

There were also a couple of brothers who evidently liked to cook, for from time to time they came to our room to seek advice, and then we could hear them banging around in the storeroom. Often they served us Jello, a perennial favorite.

Even with the diversion of cooking, the days dragged on in our new location. The weather was getting colder; the guards obligingly brought in a heater and another hot plate so we could make tea in our room. "You'll be home before Thanksgiving," they promised openly. But Ahkbar had held

---

*Army Col. Charles W. Scott, chief of the defense liaison office.
**A civilian whose occupation at the embassy was regional security officer.

182

out a similar hope when we first moved, and now we hadn't seen him for days.

Finally, a week or so before Thanksgiving, the brothers asked, "Could you fix Thanksgiving dinner?"

Ann and I talked and decided to do things up right. Thanksgiving morning, 1980, I made seven dozen donuts, and then we fixed up special decorations—turkeys made from our scraps and ingenuity—and set them on the trays with colorful leaves from the courtyard. The first course was tiny teriyaki steaks with mushroom caps and black olives. This was followed by ham steaks, candied yams, and vegetables. After dinner we sent the donuts out, and not a crumb was left over. I was exhausted, but it was good to be able to do something special again for our fellow hostages.

It seemed now that whatever was supposed to happen to help us go home had fallen through. Once more we were faced with the long prospect of more waiting. Ann had a birthday coming on December 3. Something had to be done about that.

I poked through the packs of stuff we had accumulated and found a thin, torn, faded linen napkin. *I can make a handkerchief out of that,* I thought, and sure enough, there was enough cloth for a small square. I managed to hemstitch it and to embroider an "A" for Ann in the corner when she wasn't looking.

Well, that was one thing. I also knew she loved candy, so I wrote a poem that said I would make some for her if she'd help me. I also told Ali it was her birthday and asked if he could please bring some fresh fruit.

"Yes, it can be arranged," he grinned. Sure enough, that morning the guard brought a plate of fruit—some of the most beautiful pomegranates I have ever seen—polished until they fairly glowed, and some lovely apples and oranges.

We made penuche in the afternoon, followed by a birthday dinner complete with cake decorations in the middle of the table. Mary Jane had sent me the decorations for my birthday (the package didn't arrive until December), but

183

there was no way to make a real cake in our makeshift kitchen.

December meant Christmas was approaching again, and I determined to make Christmas cards for my family early. "It takes a long time for cards to get to the States," Ann and I said when we gave the students our envelopes to mail. "Please, if we can't be home for Christmas, at least let our families have the Christmas greetings we made."

The brothers, who had been fascinated with our designs, promised to mail the cards. They also said we could write letters again. While we were pleased with the idea of being able to send mail, it was also a sign that whatever was supposed to be happening wasn't. It looked like we were going to be in Tehran for a long time yet.

And then we got a gift. One of the guards arrived with a book in hand. "You like music. Can you use this?" It was the *Lutheran Book of Worship.* "There's someone else who wants to use it, too," he warned.

"Sure," I answered eagerly. "I'd like to look at it, and then you can take it. But please bring it back so we can use it." And so, for a couple of days, the book went back and forth from one room to another. I couldn't discover where it came from or who sent it, but was it welcome! Finally, it was left with us, and Ann and I worked our way through it.

Before we knew it, the season of Advent was upon us. "Let's make an Advent wreath," I suggested. "We don't have any evergreen, but we've got candles. Let's bring some willow branches in."

We picked up red leaves in the courtyard and put those up in the room, too. A little bit of decoration, a little bit of brave color. It was time to think about another Christmas.

**Iran summons diplomats to
a discussion on hostages**
Des Moines Register
December 27, 1980

14

CHRISTMAS, 1980

The second Christmas should have been easier to handle than the first. After all, I had proved to myself the essence of Christmas was Christ, not the trappings. I had survived Christmas number one with the quiet joy of worship, filled with the strength of the Lord. I should not have the same problems in 1980. But it didn't happen that way.

It seemed to me the possibility for our release was receding. Having been moved into the prison, I was afraid the National Assembly might decide to make an example of us and put someone on trial. By this time, my suspicious nature was highly developed. I could see the macabre pleasure some of the students and their advisors would get out of executing an American "spy" on Christmas. The thought was horrid and unworthy, but it kept creeping into my mind.

I was sure we would be televised as the "guests" of the students in a festive party setting so the Iranians could once again brag about how well we were being treated. I remembered somewhat bitterly the exchange I had had with one young lady in late September.

"But we are treating you so well," she had said. "Have we not been generous? We're really not terrorists, are we?"

"Then you give me your chador and trade places with me, and try to walk out of here," I had retorted.

185

I did hope the camera would be there so my family could see I was alive and well, but I sure wasn't going to repeat the "Happy Hostage" image I had conveyed at Easter.

Ann and I differed in our opinions about Christmas dinner. I didn't want to contribute to the party atmosphere I was sure the students would try to create. She felt that if we had the chance we should do whatever we could to make our fellow hostages' day brighter. "I am willing to cook anything anytime," I told her grimly, "*except* for the TV camera."

Vainly we tried not to think about the negative things and struggled to count our blessings. We seemed to be in protective custody. The mobs that had ebbed and flowed around us for days on end while we were at the embassy were no longer near us. Ann and I were together. Our health was good. We were getting outside a little more often. We had survived longer than a year in captivity.

God had been so good about keeping us strong. Knowing I couldn't live on an eternal high, I prayed for a measure of peace and strength to help me observe this Advent properly. Perhaps celebrating the birth of the Prince of Peace, in spite of our tendency to become more discouraged at this point, would fill us with grace this Christmas.

Ann missed her family dreadfully. As an only child, she had spent most Christmases in a very traditional manner with her mother and cousins. This she had been able to continue in her adult life, and she missed it. Two years without these meaningful celebrations was a long time.

But we had to give it a try. Nothing had gotten to us yet, and neither would a second Christmas in isolation. As we lighted one, and then two candles in our Advent wreath our souls *were* strengthened. We looked forward to the quiet time of devotions each evening after dinner when we prepared aloud for the Christ Child's birth.

We also began to think about gifts. Ann was busy finishing some needlepoint to turn into an eyeglass case for her mother. I, who had never done much handiwork, was embroidering a dresser scarf for my mom and working on a needlepoint picture of Raggedy Ann for my little nieces.

186

In my only attempt to be "clever" in getting a message to my family, I mentioned in a letter that we had made our Advent wreath from willow boughs because there were no evergreen trees near us. Maybe someone would realize we had been moved, for the embassy had all sorts of pine trees on the grounds.

We started making our Christmas decorations on December 13. We hated to start, for that meant we were giving in to the idea we wouldn't be home for the holidays. I was sure we weren't going to make it, but it seemed important not to give up hope.

I folded paper and, refining my attempts from the year before, made a crèche. A tiny Christ Child wrapped in swaddling clothes, made from a bit of brown paper this year, was tucked into a manger filled with "hay" made from dried willow leaves. Mary's head cover was trimmed with a strand of blue yarn, and Joseph's head gear was held in place with black yarn taken from those precious needlepoint kits.

Whimsy took over, and two woolly lambs created from the cotton stoppers of vitamin pill bottles grazed at the foot of the manger. I knew I had a success when I handed Ann a tiny black yarn Scottish terrier and said, "Here's something to guard the sheep."

"Cinder!" she replied. "It looks just like her!" Cinder was her beloved dog back home.

At 9:30 P.M. on December 17 we were told we had ten minutes to pack. This time the brothers really meant it. We flew about the room jamming things together, trying to get our absolute necessities in one place. Fortunately, we had been living out of boxes and bags, so it was not difficult to get these things together. But we did have to dismantle the Advent wreath and the crèche, and we made one futile attempt to salvage the food from our refrigerator.

We were herded, blindfolded as always, unceremoniously into the back end of a van and driven off into the night. Even our Bibles had been taken from us, though we protested loud and long. Finally we stopped. We were warned not to talk and were led into a building, across a room, up

187

some steps and down a hallway. We heard a door open, and we were led inside. The blindfolds came off, and I looked about in amazement. We were in the entryway of what looked like a large hotel room. There was a closet, a place for luggage and (could I believe it?) to my left a *real* bathroom complete with toilet, wash basin, and *tub*! And it was clean!

"Don't turn on the lights," the brother warned, "because of the air raids. And tomorrow don't pull back the sheer curtains. You may open the drapes, but don't open the others." He started to leave.

"Where are our things?" Ann asked.

"Coming," he said and left.

It was about 10:30 P.M. We started to explore. The room was big, bigger than any we had been in before. There was a large mahogany conference table in the center, along with two straight-backed chairs upholstered in damask. One whole wall was window, with pale blue drapes, and the wallpaper was like a fine grass matting. It had obviously been elegantly appointed at one time. A pewter chandelier hung from the fifteen-feet-high ceiling, and the massive table was so highly polished it reflected even the half-light coming from the bathroom.

Evidently the plumbing had problems, for a small hole had been cut in the hall door with just enough room for two garden hoses to be pulled into the room. One ran hot water, the other cold. They had been connected to a set of faucets and that to a shower head. Theoretically, at least, we had running hot and cold water. We set about ignoring minor details—connections that leaked and lack of pressure—and savored the thought of having toilet, laundry, and bathing facilities to use at our discretion. What luxury.

Our things still did not come. "Let's exercise," Ann suggested. There was room to *run* here, and we did. Midnight arrived, and then twelve-thirty. Still no clothes, no bedding, no Bibles.

Ann banged on the door. "Where are our things?" she began. "We'd like to sleep."

"Coming," responded the brother, and we waited some more. Finally at 2:00 A.M. we each received a blanket, not the ones we had been using, and nothing else. We curled up on the floor and slept.

The next morning about 8:00 our stuffed pillowcases and two mattresses arrived. Our Bibles were untouched. "Thank You, God." We started to unpack. Good grief! There were even hangers in the closet! How we laughed as we stowed our pitiful garments in this spacious room.

Ann grew very quiet as she dug deeper and deeper into her bag. "You know what those so-and-so's took?" she finally burst out, her eyes flashing. "My grape jelly!" She had used it only sparingly and had been saving it for months.

About that time there was a knock at the door. As the brother handed us glasses of tea, bread, and grape jelly, he said, "We're awfully glad you had all that jelly. We didn't know what we were going to give you for breakfast." We didn't know whether to laugh or to cry.

"I just hope *our* guys got some!" Ann said.

I counted up: This was the thirteenth time I had been moved. We settled into our routine again, only this time with an alarm clock of sorts, the school girls next door. Our enormous plate glass window looked onto the back of a girls' school, and the students there started each day doing calisthenics and yelling political slogans.

It was time to decorate our new room. We had had to leave our Advent wreath of willow branches behind; but, digging about in our bags, we discovered a piece of green tinsel left over from the previous year. It made a great wreath. The candles were put back in place, and the effect on the table was splendid. The crèche went on a small cabinet to one side, and the snowflakes I had used the year before were pinned on the wall above the crèche. In the center of the wall arrangement was the metallic star I had been given in 1979.*

---

*Though I had left it behind on one move, I had found it in the rubbish later in the year and rescued it.

189

Ann took one look at the figures I had made for the crèche and set to work. Soon we had a dozen or more small angels standing guard near our Advent wreath, at the crèche, and on our bookshelves. The colored insides of envelopes made their skirts, strands of yarn their heads, and carefully saved aluminum foil their wings and arms. The Christmas cards we had received the year before marched across the cabinet tops. It almost felt like home when we basked in the warmth of the sunny window or watched the snow as it fell slowly to the ground.

By this time I had lost so much weight I had taken in my blue trousers. I cut the scraps of blue from the seams into bookmark-size strips, and on each I embroidered a symbol: a cross with a sunburst behind it for Ann, a "Chi Rho"* to have on hand and perhaps give to the priest should one be permitted to come. I made a pen and pencil holder out of a toilet paper tube, covering it with an old envelope, and another bookmark in gold paper from an old greeting card. It would be a slim Christmas.

On December 23 one of the brothers showed up bright and early. "It's your turn to prepare things," he directed, setting down two thirty-gallon bags full of greens. He left and returned quickly with two large pots. Breakfast came hard on his heels.

Ann and I dumped the greens into the tub, ran it full of water, and then ate our breakfast. I'm not sure quite how it happened, but those two bags of greens seemed to grow while we were washing them. We washed and cleaned and sorted and picked for hours—six, to be exact. We were exhausted by the end of the day.

Air raids were occurring with increasing frequency, so we decided to leave the light in the main room off after dusk and sit on the floor in the entryway during the evening. That

---

*The first two Greek letters in the word "Christ," superimposed one over the other, is a well-known religious symbol in liturgical churches.

way we were also closer to the bathroom, which had no windows. If the situation grew really dangerous, we could duck in there and be out of the path of flying glass.

We continued to have our evening devotions around our Advent wreath. The glory of that quiet time, as the light of the candles reflected in dancing beams on the tinsel and tiny angel wings, was such a balm. We lingered over singing hymns and carols, reading Scripture, and remembering our families in prayer. During those quiet times God was so close we truly were in a place apart.

Finally, all four candles were lighted. The following day would be Christmas Eve. We knelt for one last moment, then blew out the candles and moved to the entryway for our evening reading.

Before long one of the brothers knocked, and we opened the door. Looking rather uncomfortable, he began a little speech. "Tomorrow you celebrate your Christmas. Will you get your room ready for a party? We will bring you a tree and decorations. Will you arrange it so it looks nice? It must be ready by 6:00 p.m."

"Let's see what you have," I said quietly.

More brothers came in carrying boxes. "If you need anything, tell us," one said on the way out.

"Looks like the old propaganda routine," I said wryly.

"I expect so," Ann added. "Only this time I'm not going to play into their hands. No jolly holly time from me."

"Nor me," I agreed wholeheartedly. "But if we don't decorate, they will. Let's do it our way."

We started digging through the boxes, much of which had obviously been rifled from the embassy co-op. First we set up the tree. It was artificial, but pretty. It could stand in the corner. Then there were boxes of red ribbons and white ribbons and one box of huge yellow bows. We grinned. Did the students know anything about the yellow ribbons? "Let's just put *one* on the tree," Ann said. "Right where it *can't* be missed!"

"We can tear some of these apart and make gold chains,"

191

I said. "This stuff sticks to itself." We got busy planning decorations. Ann reached for the foil and began shaping tiny animals for the tree. I got out our pack rat bag and sorted green and red and gold envelopes. Before too long it was midnight, and we had a star-cross for the top of the tree, a dozen tiny reindeer, an "Alpha and Omega," and several snowflakes. My fingers ached from cutting thin strips of foil to make icicles.

Morning light brought more supplies. A tiny tree was decorated with the resurrected "Easter eggs" we had used in April and put in one corner. A carton of stuffed Santas arrived, and while we didn't think much of them, the boxes they were in looked like row upon row of townhouses, so a little village took shape under the tree.

Red ribbons were used to decorate the doors and the chandelier. The room looked festive but not overdone.

At 5:30 one of the brothers showed up. "We have a real tree for you," he announced, displaying a huge, fragrant pine.

"It's too late!" I wailed. "We were told we had to be ready by six! Wait—can you cut some branches off the bottom?" I wasn't going to let that pine escape completely.

"Sure," he said. "How much do you want?"

"Lots," I said recklessly.

We got it!

About that time the brother we called Honcho (because he seemed to be the head man around) also came in, looked around, and sniffed. He left. "Doesn't like what we did," said Ann.

"Let's set these greens about. That'll help," I suggested. And we flew around making swags of greenery tied with red ribbons to decorate every bare space there was, and deliberately we decided to wear yellow headbands in our hair.

In the midst of our finishing touches a heavy air bombardment started. The noise of gunfire and bombs grew closer and closer, until we finally made a dive for the bathroom, flashing off the lights on the way. We nearly knocked down one of the brothers arriving with our dinner. He simply laughed at our fright, assuring us we didn't need to worry. It was all I could do to refrain from snapping back, "If I weren't locked in a room, perhaps I wouldn't be frightened either!"

The 6:00 deadline had long passed. We ate our dinner and wondered what would happen. I stopped Honcho when he returned momentarily. "Excuse me, but I would like to ask that we be allowed to worship with our colleagues. I know you've said we couldn't be together in the past because it wouldn't look good and people would talk. They can hardly talk about our being with the men for church services in the presence of a priest, can they?"

"That would be very difficult for the men," he began predictably. "You must understand our problems."

"But I think you should understand that part of Christian worship is fellowship. Coming together as one body is very important to us, especially at times like Christmas and Easter."

"We'll see," he said, and that was all. The brothers returned shortly, and Ann and I picked up our blankets, our Bibles, and some books to read and were lead down the hall. The time was 9:30 P.M. We were ushered into a small butler's pantry and there we sat, listening to the groups of men being led down the hall to our room. Each time we heard "Silent Night" being sung we had to suppose it was a new worship service.

About midnight a brother brought us each a dish of pudding: chocolate and vanilla. We ate part of it and shifted around in our chairs. The seats were hard, and there was no heat. *Don't think about going home. Don't think about being discouraged,* I told myself. *You're going to see a priest and have an opportunity to worship.* Finally at 1:30 A.M., we were told it was our turn. We collected our Bibles and books, allowed blindfolds to be tied in place, and were led down the hall.

Once in our room, the blindfolds came off and there was our old friend, the papal nuncio, Monsignor Anibale Bugnini, and another priest. They greeted us warmly. I glanced quickly around the room. Blinding TV lights and cameras, brothers all over the place, and extra chairs—eight of them. The men must have been in groups of six. The remains of cakes, pies, jello, pudding, and fresh fruit were everywhere. Crumbs all over the carpet. Had the men been able to leave us any signs? Tomorrow's job would be cleaning up the mess, but right now the order was worship.

The nuncio asked us to seat ourselves on either side of the priest. We did so and the worship began. We sang "Silent Night," and I read the words of prophecy from Isaiah. We stumbled along as best we could, saying the words of the Nicene Creed in a new English version. Bishop John Issayi gave a homily. He chose to speak to us about Mary and how she served the Lord.

Then he began Communion. As the words of the service were read, I thought back to the longing I had had in March and how a spiritual communion had served me for so many months. Silently, I thanked the Lord for the gift of His sacrament and gratefully received the wafer from the bishop.

Then the nuncio did a most unusual thing. He leaned over and spoke to the priest, and Bishop Issayi lifted the chalice and presented it to me. I drank as tears of gratitude filled my eyes. When would I have Communion again? I didn't know.

The worship service finished, and we spoke briefly to the visitors. The priest handed each of us a tiny crucifix. Then I went over to the tree, where two of my bookmarks were hanging, and shyly handed one to each of them. My offering was so humble. They accepted with joy.

Then the inevitable. "Would you like to say something to your families?"

"You first, Kate," said Ann.

I remembered all the advice I had given my speech class students for years. Two deep breaths. I would not break down on camera! My knees and legs were trembling. I pressed my hands down hard and fought for inner control. I needed every remnant I could muster.

194

One more deep breath, and I began. Would it work? Would the students film all I wanted to say and do? I had thought about this for hours on end. When I had been small, about five years old, there had been a kidnapping and brutal murder of a child about my age. I had been terrified, even though the tragedy had taken place in another state. I was terribly worried that my own nieces and nephews might be having problems coping with what had happened to Aunt Kate. This was for them and for Mother, Father, my sisters, and their husbands.

"I want to thank you, Mother and Daddy," I began "for everything you have taught me about love and life, both life on this earth and in eternity.

"Jared, Suzie, Carrie, Diann, John Lars, Becky, Mark, and Emma Lou, can you sing with me?" I took another deep breath and began to sing softly the third verse of "Away in a Manger."

Be near me, Lord Jesus!
I ask Thee to stay
Close by me forever,
And love me, I pray.

Bless all the dear children
In Thy tender care,
And take us to heaven,
To live with Thee there.

"I'm fine," I added. "I continue to lose weight, which makes me happy." And I finished off my comments.

"Dear Lord," I prayed silently, "let the students send this so my family can see it." Anabeth had written after Easter that they had gone to the TV studio and looked at the clips sent by the students. I prayed this one would get through to my family.

Ann spoke to her family, and the priests began to pack up to leave. Monsignor Bugnini asked if he could have mementos from the tree to take to the Foreign Office to Bruce, Vic, and Mike. Another gift! The men were still there.

The students brought us each a package of letters, a warm-up outfit and a jacket, and a game. The priest left, blindfolded, and we began to clean up the debris.

Our mattresses reappeared, and we settled down to our nighttime routine. I glanced at the mail. That I would save for the next day. I had to wake up before Ann so I could stuff her stocking. We had each pinned a stocking to the wall near the tree. I had some hard candies hoarded away and the bookmark. There was the pencil holder to dig out and slip under the tree, too. Finally we slept.

Christmas Day we rose late, breakfasted, and then had our worship service. I deliberately chose to read, for our "sermon," a selection from Edna Hong's *Bright Valley of Love*. Before I started I handed Ann a wad of Kleenex.

"Here," I said. "We're going to have a good cry."

I read a selection about handicapped children and how one of them learned about Christmas. We cried for them and for us. It felt so good!

After that, we took down our stockings. I had one filled with things Ann had hoarded, and she had similar goodies from me. She loved the pencil holder, and the mobile she had made for me was smashing. I promptly hung it from the chandelier, where it moved about making an ever-changing pattern.

We had barely settled into our reading when the brothers came with more gifts. Candy and snacks from our diplomatic colleagues in Tehran. Perfume from Ahkbar! Books—I recognized the titles as those I had asked for when I wrote Dr. Preus September 3. The first one, a Bible commentary, was one I had hoped would come for Ann's birthday. She got it for Christmas instead.

Later in the day we each got a shoe box of presents from our families, and that evening two representatives from the Algerian Embassy came to visit. They had a long check list of people who were supposed to be in our building, but they could tell us only that negotiations were underway. They left, and we were alone.

196

We ate a piece of chocolate and thought of the bittersweet day that had passed. We had celebrated another Christmas in Iran, as prisoners. Yet, as we lighted the Christmas candle in the center of our Advent wreath, we knew it had been just as hard on our families as it had been on us. The Algerians had seen us; the ministers had, too. The TV camera had been there: We hoped our families would know we were holding up.

"What would you like to sing?" I asked, holding the hymnal.

"Angels We Have Heard on High," said Ann, and the strains of "Gloria" filled our hearts and room.

**Execution of hostages is
threatened by Iran**
Des Moines Register
January 1, 1981

15

JANUARY, 1981

We were determined to bring in the new year with noise. Somehow the idea of spending a full calendar year in captivity seemed more awful than the mere passing of 365 days in that state. So, promptly at midnight Tehran time, we banged on the wall that separated our room from the men next door. It was lovely: They banged right back. Happy New Year! One more small triumph.

I had made Ann a card, and on New Year's morning, I gave it to her. It was a little snowman: Cotton balls to make his body, twigs from our evergreen branches to make his arms, and yarn for his scarf. His features and top hat I sketched in with pen and ink. Inside was a short poem:

> It shouldn't be too difficult
>   To make a New Year's rhyme;
> As I sit here in my palace cell
>   I have a lot of time.
>
> I'll write a New Year's wish
>   For a change in situation
> (And add a little note of thanks that
>   "nistie"* aggravation,

Nist is the Farsi word for "there isn't any." The sisters used it constantly, often to avoid getting things for us.

198

Developed by our "hohars"
has gone its quiet way)
So here's to Happy New Year
Beginning with today!

May your year be filled with joy
May it shine in all that's good
May it find you back in G'town
And in New Hampshire's wood

May it bring you all your friends
With lots of happy wishes
And parties fraught with fun
And all your favorite dishes

May it be a year for you
When all is said and done
That's exactly what you'd like
God's year, Nineteen eighty-one!

The days following New Year's were more of the same: study, read, think, pray. As I was reading First and Second Corinthians, I was struck by how important it was that I should be looking at everyone in a manner befitting a child of God. That eliminated judging others from a human point of view, and that meant accepting each one in the present as he or she is, including the students. There was food for thought!

I was especially grateful for the books that I was reading. A little volume called *Appointment in Jerusalem* depicted the strong faith one woman had. In one place she said, "Trust is a decision." I thought about that statement, and I decided I could trust in the Lord. I could trust Him to use me and to use this situation.

Believing that God was using me right then was difficult, however, when so little was going on. There seemed to be no way I could help anyone other than Ann, and that was easy because she was helping me. Our life in captivity really had been easier when we could do something like cooking. Now all we could do was continue with our program of exercise and wonder if this stalemate would ever be resolved.

The students brought a videotape machine to the center

199

where we were being detained, and we saw a couple of films: *Circus of the Stars* and a Barbra Streisand movie, *What's Up, Doc?* (I thought the latter was as silly in Iran as it was the first time I saw it.) I began to have trouble sleeping. I thought it might be the foam mattress, so I slept on the floor one night and that seemed to be better. There was a warm spot on the floor where hot water pipes ran underneath.

The Iran-Iraq war was taking its toll. The electricity was off regularly, at times twice a day. There were changes in guards, and some of the students were gone. Ahkbar, we learned, had gone off to report on the war for one of the news agencies. We depended on the girls in the school yard behind us to keep us up on current hostilities. They shouted *"Marg bar Ahm-ri-ka"* or *"Marg bar Schu-ra-vie* ("Death to Russia") as current events dictated.

Then, on Saturday, January 17, Honcho came to say we might be going home very soon.

"Look, don't tell us until we're ready to go!" we interrupted. "You've done this to us now for six weeks, and we don't want to hear it unless you're ready to take us home."

He stopped in mid-sentence and said, "Well . . ." and left the room. We didn't know whether to believe him or not, so we tried to put what he had said out of our minds and carry on with our regular routines. The rest of that day and Sunday passed quietly. But early on Monday morning there was a knock on the door.

"Yes?" I replied.

"May we come in?"

"Certainly," I said, grabbing for my caftan, a birthday present from an unknown well-wisher. "Just a moment."

A brother entered, closing the door behind him. "We have a surprise for you. We have someone here to see you." Ann and I looked at each other and ran our fingers through our hair. Who could be coming? The brother opened the door, and there stood Tiger Lily.

Our reception of her was hardly what they had expected. Coolly each of us said the traditional Farsi greeting. "Good morning. How are you?" Finally we did ask her to sit.

200

I could not get terribly excited about seeing her. She had lied to us often and had attempted to pass off the flimsiest of rhetorical propaganda, expecting us to believe her. Ann and I felt that the sisters had forfeited many of their rights to deal with us because of their constant deference to the brothers and their inability to do anything on their own.

Tiger Lily began with great formality. "We are not one hundred percent certain you will be released, but let me tell you that it has never been so close nor so real." She stopped for effect. We were stone-faced. "Negotiations are underway, and the possibility exists that you will be released."

She talked for a few more minutes. We listened silently to what she had to say and said thank you when she left.

A short time later another brother came in. "There will be Algerian doctors coming to examine you." We thanked him, and he left. Finally, one of the students came in. "Get a few things together. We want to take you to another room."

"Are we leaving here for good?" we asked.

"No, no. We just need to use your room."

We put together the books we were reading, our Bibles and needlework, and were led blindfolded to the familiar little room we had been kept in at Christmastime. It was very tiny and cramped. But there was room for two chairs, and somebody brought blankets. We settled in and speculated about what was going on.

Before too long, a brother came back and said, "We want to interview you for our archives." I looked at Ann. We knew what this meant: propaganda. Silently we put on our blindfolds and were led back to our room.

As we expected, everything had been very carefully rearranged. Our two chairs were moved back into one corner with a small table in front of them, decorated with our miniature Christmas tree. On the radiator behind the "set" were amassed every Christmas card from our room that they could find. Ann was as angry as I was, I knew. We really resented our room being used in this way. We sat on the chairs, and Tiger Lily came in. She sat facing us with her back to the television camera.

201

"We'd like to talk about your treatment while you were here," she began. "We want you to tell us about the food, about the care you received, how you were treated, what your feelings were like."

Just as we had thought. Ann and I had discussed the possibility of such an interview, and we weren't going to make it easy for the students. We had decided we were not going to make them sound good when we didn't think they had been, while being as honest as we could be.

Ann spoke first. "Physically, we have been treated quite well. We have had plenty of food to eat; we are warm. But we have been afraid the entire time we've been here. We have not always had the mail from our families that you told us we would have. Sometimes, months have gone by without letters from our parents," she elaborated.

We took turns talking about not being able to exercise, the infrequency of baths, the limited trips outside, and not being permitted to speak to our colleagues.

At one point, when the tape was being changed, Tiger Lily challenged us. "You're being very negative. You might talk about some of the positive things that happened."

"Can you tell me one positive thing about being locked up?" I snapped.

She shrugged her shoulders as if to rid herself of a mild irritation. "But what about the treats? What about the nuts? What about the goodies?"

The cameraman interrupted to tell her they were ready to roll, so she resumed her position and continued the interview. After forty-five minutes we were dismissed.

Blindfolded, we were led back to the butler's pantry. We barely had time to compare notes when three men who looked like a medical team came in. They were dressed in white coats and carried a tray of vials and utensils. Assuming they were Algerian, I began to speak to them in French. They couldn't answer me. They were Iranian. I called the brother and declared that since they were not Algerian, they were not going to touch me. I had expected to see Algerian medical doctors. Ann said nothing.

202

After several minutes of verbal battling, Honcho arrived.

"What are you talking about? You will not be released until you've talked to these people."

"You told us that this was an Algerian medical team. These are not Algerians; they are Iranians. What happened to the Algerian doctors? What is this group of people doing here?"

Honcho was livid, and we exchanged more words. Finally, I capitulated. "Of course, I'm your *prisoner.* You can do with me what you want." Ann and I consented to let them take the blood samples they needed. We could see that their equipment was packaged and thus sterile. Then, our Bibles in hand, we were directed downstairs to a room where another team of doctors waited, this time Algerians.

The same tall, well-dressed student who had talked with me in perfect English at the outset of this ordeal, and who I had hoped was from the Foreign Ministry, was in the examination room also, with several Iranian news photographers. The photographers took several quick pictures and slipped out, but "Scarecrow," as we had nicknamed him, seemed settled in for the duration.

"He must leave if you are to examine me," I said to the doctor.

Scarecrow tried a conciliatory smile. "Now, Miss Koob, you know better than that. . ."

"Listen, if you want one of the sisters here so that you have a student present, that's fine. But you will not be in this room while I am examined."

"Miss Koob. . ."

"Look!" I said sharply. "You're not a medical doctor. If these doctors are to do an examination, you will leave. I will not have an examination with a man in the room."

His face smoothed into a hard mask, but he went and got one of the sisters. Another small triumph.

As soon as he left, the doctors began their examination. My French was very rusty, but I managed to convey to them that I could understand most of what they were saying, even though I could not respond much beyond *oui* or *non.*

203

The exam was thorough, followed by an electrocardiogram given in another room by young female technicians. Finally, it was over. Still hanging onto our Bibles, Ann and I were led back upstairs to the pantry.

The guard had had trouble with my blindfold and impatiently had just thrown my scarf over my head. As we passed through the corridors, I could see clearly a number of our colleagues coming and going with their guards. There were so many of them! They all looked to be in good shape, as if they had survived well. Was our ordeal really coming to an end? Could we really be going home? I dared not let myself think about it.

For the first time since we had been taken hostage, Ann and I were given back issues of the *Teheran Times*, an Iranian government paper. The headline stories were about the negotiations. Was what we read only propaganda for public consumption, or was there really something there to believe? Ann and I didn't know what to think. After all the other false hopes, we determined to remain neutral.

We sat in the pantry for hours and hours, listening to the hustle and bustle in the halls. At 9:00 P.M. a brother stuck his head in the door. "You can't be very comfortable in this room."

"No, we're not."

"Get your things together," he said. "We've found another place for you. Sorry, but we're still using your room."

We put our blindfolds on and were taken to a kitchen, where two comfortable chairs obviously had been hastily brought in. The brothers left us alone, and we began to look around.

All kinds of things were piled on the shelves. The cupboards were filled with paper products and other items from the embassy co-op: cleaning supplies, foodstuffs, toiletries, as well as potato chips and snack foods. And there, tossed up on the very top, was mail! Package after package that had never been delivered.

Ann and I simply were beyond anger. Carefully we took

down the boxes and opened them. There was a sweatshirt for somebody. Another box contained a Bible. There was a book mailer from Augsburg Publishing House with a wrapping like those we had received at Christmas. It was all so senseless! Someone could have been keeping warm with that shirt. Someone could have been reading those letters and that Bible.

We pulled the Augsburg package off the shelf and discovered it was the daily devotional booklet I had asked Dr. Preus to send. Determinedly we took the book out of the wrapping and put the empty paper back up on the shelf. Our devotional lessons would be secure!

The students began to come in for odd items or snacks, and by 1:30 we could see the exhaustion on their faces. It had been a tough and strenuous day for all of us. Shortly we heard the clank of equipment moving down the hall, and a brother arrived. "You must be exhausted," he said. "You can go back to your room now."

Blindfolded and weary, we stumbled back to our room, which was littered with crumbs and leftovers from the students' snacking. The little table was gone, and the two straight-backed chairs were in place. Our mattresses and blankets were returned so we could sleep.

We slept fitfully and were awakened early by the school girls. The activities of the day before must have taken the starch out of our captors, for the hall was quiet and breakfast was very, very late. We dug into our supplies being kept cool at the edge of the window and brought out some dates. This inauspicious start could mean a *very* long day!

Then the drums started under the window. Thump . . . thump . . . thump. The beat was slow, dolorous, a mourning sound, and it seemed as if it would go on for hours. The students began marching and chanting as well, to the slow cadence of that lugubrious drum.

The skies were leaden. "I don't expect we'll hear anything till 6:30 or so," I said to Ann.

"What do you mean?"

"It's Inauguration Day," I said. "I think the ceremony takes place at 10:30, Washington time. If we hear anything, it'll be 6:30 this evening."

"I expect you're right" was all she said. We went back to our reading. The day was gray, dismal. Thump . . . thump . . . thump went the drum in the background.

**Hostages free at last
as Reagan takes office**
Des Moines Register
January 21, 1981

16

JANUARY 20, 1981

I remember the details exactly.

It was ten minutes to six when one of the brothers came to the door and knocked. He entered the room and, with a piece of paper in his hands, said, "Get ready. We are going."

"Going where?" Ann asked.

"To the United States," he answered. "Get your things ready."

We did not even exchange glances. Instead, we reached into the cupboard with one accord and pulled out the getaway bags that had been ready for months. It all took five, maybe ten seconds. "We're ready. Let's go."

He stared at us, shocked. After a moment he found his voice. "We'll be back in less than an hour," he said, and turned and left.

Now Ann and I stared at each other, fear and hope reflected in our eyes. "Do you suppose this is really happening?" she asked. We had learned from the Algerian ambassador that negotiations were underway; we had been examined by Algerian doctors; and it was Inauguration Day. The signs were right, but we also knew we could not trust the students. This could simply be another ruse to move us and conveniently "lose" some of our belongings.

207

We immediately began to double-dress, putting on extra pairs of jeans we each had salvaged from the trash and an extra sweater. Then we went through our meager belongings, carefully gathering up the items we particularly wanted to take with us in case we *weren't* going home. We tied our Bibles together so the papers and photos would not fall out. In the midst of all the rush, the lights went out. Ann and I simply laughed. How typical. We grabbed our matches and lit candles.

After a few minutes, another brother came in. "You can't take all that," he said. "It's too much. Just take one small package."

"Wait," I said. "These are letters you gave me from my family. I want to take them home."

"Nobody got that much mail," he snapped as he left the room.

Hastily I repacked the letters neatly with my needlework and tucked in the little angels we had made at Christmas. Finally, we made our bags small enough to satisfy the brother. He stormed back into the room saying, "Why aren't you ready? You'll never get to go if you don't leave immediately."

"We are ready," I said. "Here are our blindfolds."

We were marched by several brothers through the corridor and down the steps to a lower level entrance. The blast of cold air from outside felt exhilarating. As we stepped out, someone said, "Be careful. There is ice underfoot." Then came a conversation to see if we should be put on the waiting bus. No, it was full.

We could tell from the noise of the motors that there were several vehicles in the yard. Finally, two brothers led Ann and me to a vehicle and told us to step up. I put my hand out awkwardly. It touched a guardrail, and I grabbed it and pulled myself in. Then Ann and I were side by side, she on my left, on a long bench seat. I could sense there were other people around us, and the students warned, "Don't esspeak."

How I longed to believe we were really going home! Yet I

208

held myself tightly in reserve. I knew something was different, because for the first time we were in the same vehicle with the male hostages. I became aware of a man seated to my right.

"How are you?" he probed quietly after a moment.

"Fine. Who is it?" I answered.

"Kalp."

"It's Koob," I said.

It was Malcolm Kalp, an embassy officer. Voices of the students came at us: "Sh-sh, don't esspeak."

We sat for what seemed an eternity in silence, waiting, but for what? I lost track of time. I hadn't remembered to look at our Rolex when we left the room. An American in the back made a derogatory remark in Farsi to one of the guards and was immediately pulled off the van and beaten. We could hear the sickening thuds of the blows. I was afraid he would not be allowed back in the van, but finally we heard him being shoved into his seat.

At last, the bus lurched ahead. We seemed to be traveling mostly in a straight line. As we bounced awkwardly on the seats, I strained to pick up familiar voices.

After about thirty minutes, the bus came to a halt. "You can take your blindfolds off now," the driver announced. Floodlights and a huge full moon illuminated our surroundings. We were at the Tehran airport!

I looked around. There was Mike Metrinko at the back of the bus. I thought I had recognized his voice. He definitely looked as if he had been roughed up. And Bob Blucker. And Malcolm, next to me. We began to talk in snatches, carefully because the students were still with us.

A number of military guards were strolling around outside, rifles casually in hand. Ahead of us was a large bus, packed with our colleagues. As I watched, they were taken from the bus one by one and escorted past a chanting, jeering mob of students, in the blinding glare of television camera lights, to the planes. Only then did I see the pair of Algerian airliners, waiting sleek and poised on the tarmac.

209

Was this really happening? The students were still chanting, their fists in the air: *"Marg bar Ahm-ri-ka. Marg bar Car-tare."* And now, a new chant: *"Marg bar Ray-gan."*

It was time for our van to be emptied. One by one they hustled us over to the planes. As I stepped out, I saw little Ali to my right. But then I was overwhelmed by the sea of bearded faces, all shouting *"Marg bar Ahm-ri-ka!"* one last time and shaking their fists. "These guys aren't going to get me now!" I said to myself determinedly. I raised my chin to show my pride for our country and let myself be escorted to the plane in front of this ragtail crowd.

I walked up the ramp of the plane hardly knowing what to expect. Inside the plane I had to push through a small clump of Iranian newsmen and cameras. Then the most beautiful sight of all: My colleagues—standing, cheering, and clapping—greeting each new arrival.

There was Bruce Laingen. And right beside him, my boss, John Graves. In front of John were Barry Rosen and Bill Royer, saving a seat for me between them.

We grabbed each other with great wordless hugs, and the conversation dam broke.

"How are you?"

"I'm fine. Are you OK?"

"I'm great!"

I sat down, beginning now to talk a mile a minute.

"Were you taken out of Tehran?"

"How about that last place? It was something!"

"Did you see the room with the crystal chandeliers?"

"You know the room with the Christmas tree? That was Ann's and my room!"

Among those on board were the Algerian ambassador to Iran who had visited us at Christmas and a gentleman someone identified as the Swiss ambassador, Erik Lang. They were there with a list, asking us to sign in, checking off names. While they took census, I took off my extra layer of clothes and listened to Don Cooke tell how he hid his class ring so the students wouldn't find it.

Vaguely I heard someone pleading, "People, you've got to sit down and buckle up your seat belts or we won't be able to take off!" But I was talking so much I never even felt us taxi down the runway. What a grand and glorious feeling to be on that plane!

Bruce had asked the captain to let us know when we left Iranian air space. When the announcement finally came, there was a deafening cheer and from somewhere Algerian Airlines produced champagne to help us celebrate our freedom. In return, we signed a copy of the daily newspaper for each of the crew members. Only then did I realize how tense I still was. In the back of my mind I had known we could be turned around while still in Iranian air space. Personally, I halfway expected us to be fired on once we were over Turkey. The students had often claimed the CIA wanted us dead. With their revolutionary paranoia and obsession with super-spy tactics, it would not have surprised me if the students had tried to blow us out of the sky and put the blame on the CIA.

But for now, everyone was celebrating. The Algerians apologized for not having a meal for us, but no one seemed to care. I would learn later they had gone to a market in Tehran and bought bread and cheese to make the snack they served us. They had taken their responsibility seriously. The military guard we had seen at the airport were *Algerian* guards sent to watch the planes while we were in neutral custody.

Originally they told us we would stop in Turkey, but plans changed, and we set down in Athens. When we touched the runway, I finally, truly relaxed. *We'll get home now.* I knew a U.S. military base was nearby and that we'd have an escort if needed. We were free!

From Athens to Algeria, it was more talk, talk, talk, all of us wide awake into the night. There was so much to be said, and it was *so* good to be back together.

By the time the plane touched down in Algiers, we were impatient, wanting to go on home.

"Why don't we get on to Frankfurt?"

"Let's just go home!"

"We don't need these hassles!"

The murmuring in the ranks threatened mutiny.

But we listened respectfully when Algerian officials came on board and gave us our instructions. There would be a receiving line. We then would proceed to the airport lounge, where we would officially be turned over to the American government officials who were there. Each of us had to be given an identification card so we could be presented properly.

Finally somebody said, "OK, let's go!" Then the cry went up. "Ladies first!"

Ann and I moved toward the front of the line, but Ann was calling, "Where's Bruce? We won't go without Bruce!"

Bruce called to us from the back. "I'm going to be the last one off. The captain leaves the ship last."

We protested. "No. You're the leader. We won't get off unless you come with us. You lead us off."

Everyone else agreed. We waited for Bruce, and with Ann and me on either side of him, we trooped victoriously out the doorway. But we had taken no more than a step or two when Bruce put Ann's and my hands together, moved us forward, and dropped back a step behind us.

There were television lights and cameras and all kinds of people waiting to greet us. I was surprised to see that many of them were crying. People I had never seen before were embracing us, the tears streaming down their cheeks. But no one was more beautiful than Ulrich Haynes, our American ambassador to Algeria, and his wife as they met us with hugs and tears.

On we walked. People lined the airport fence, cheering, and there were more lights and cameras. How crazy: It was 1:30 in the middle of the night! I had no idea this was live TV coverage!

We entered the reception room to find rows of chairs in two different areas, one to the right and one to the left. We all moved toward the chairs and sat down. Eventually the official welcoming party began to assemble. While we sat there waiting, a TV reporter asked, "Does anybody want to say anything?"

They poked a long mike in my face. I said, "It's good to be going home," and the cameras passed on.

Then I remembered those long days in Tehran. One of the things I had said I wanted to do if I had the chance was to say thank you to all the people who had prayed for us. So I called to the cameraman and said, "Excuse me, may I say something else?" He came back quickly. "The one thing I would like to say to everybody at home is, you can never imagine how much your letters, your prayers, and support meant to us. We were unable to write to you or to communicate with you; only the Lord knows how much it helped. Thank you from the bottom of my heart."

He moved on, and I felt I had kept a promise.

The ceremonies began. An official statement was read, first by a representative of the government of Algeria, and then by Mr. Warren Christopher from our State Department. After 444 long days we were no longer hostages but free Americans, ready to continue on what had begun to be known as our "flight to freedom."

Back outside again, a light drizzle was blackening the tarmac. Filing out to the planes for the next leg of the journey, how I wished we were not going to Frankfurt but to the United States of America! We boarded two American Red Cross Nightingales, with that lovely American flag painted on their tails. Inside, big "Welcome to Freedom" signs and yellow ribbons greeted us everywhere. Each seat was sporting a bow, and the Air Force crew all wore them, too.

We were given current magazines: *Time*, *Newsweek*, even *Playboy*. I snuggled into the big seat and began to read and catch up on what was going on. I discovered that would take a while!

With fewer people on the plane, I could talk more easily to my colleagues. One of the U.S. government people I had met for the first time in Algiers said to me, "Kate, you have

213

super parents. They are the salt of the earth." The man was Sheldon Krys, the State Department officer who had had the most regular contact with my parents during the crisis. He went on to tell me that Mary Jane had done an outstanding job as spokesperson for our family. He could count on her whenever something needed to be said.

"You have no idea what's waiting for you all when you get home!" Sheldon continued. "You simply cannot understand what sort of welcome has been planned for you and how the American public feels about you." I had little idea how true his words were.

Koob: "I'm fine; thank you
for your prayers"
Des Moines Register
January 22, 1981

17
JANUARY 21, 1981

When the planes landed in Rhein-Main, West Germany, I put on my new Air Force parka, which was warm and had a million pockets, and I pinned the yellow ribbon from the plane seat on the front of it. I grabbed my bundle, and we stepped off the plane to another reception line and more television cameras.

The first person I saw was Harry Barnes, director general of the foreign service, who had been my ambassador in Romania when I was assistant cultural affairs attaché there. I gave him a big hug. Next I saw my boss from Washington, Ted Curran. As I hugged him he said, "How are you, Kate?"

My answer was "I'm fine, Ted. What's my next job?" And I was serious!

We boarded the sleek, modern buses that were to take us to the American military hospital in nearby Wiesbaden. I was tired—but not too tired to talk! Ambassador Barnes sat down beside me, and we began to catch up: What was going on in Romania and how Betsy, his wife, was; my experiences in Tehran, and how, while I had been captive, my faith had been so important.

We had been told on the planes there would be telephones waiting for us at the hospital. What we hadn't been

215

told was that the German nation would be out to greet us as well as almost every American living between the airport and the hospital.

As the buses negotiated through traffic, we began to get some sense of what was in store for us. Cars were stopped all along the roadway, and people had gotten out of them, all waving, applauding, and shouting. I couldn't believe all the commotion was for us, but Harry insisted it was. I had expected our colleagues in the foreign service to be delighted, but I had no idea that everyone else in the world had been so caught up in what had happened to us.

We had another dose of excitement when we arrived at the hospital. Hundreds of people were crowded on the porches and lining the walks, cheering and clapping, and more television cameras and news crews were everywhere. Still a bit stunned, we waved and smiled and disappeared into the hospital.

We were taken to the third floor, where a special wing had been set up for us. The hospital superintendent greeted us warmly and assured us the news people would be kept outside the hospital area for the four or five days we would be there for tests. It was suggested that we not leave the hospital grounds, but the gates were open. We were free Americans once again, and we could do as we wished.

Someone also told us where the telephones were, gave us our room assignments, and checked us in. I went down to my room and dumped my things. Ann appeared from somewhere. In amazement, we examined the goodies on the bedside tables: shampoo, face cream, makeup—all the things we had rarely seen in Tehran. Our room even had a hot shower—and lots of towels! And our beds were actually on legs! We laughed and almost cried. Then we made a beeline for the telephone.

We were too late. Other people had gotten there first, so we patiently took our place in line. At that point a Dr. Johnson introduced himself. He was to be my psychiatrist during my stay at Wiesbaden. We talked briefly and informally

216

about some of the things that had helped me deal with the situation in Iran, and then it was my turn on the telephone. Because it was January, I was quite sure my parents were no longer in Iowa. I decided to call Mary Jane.

It was 3:17 in the morning, Washington time, when the telephone rang, but her husband John answered, not "hello" but "Hello, Kate!" He yelled for Janie. We exchanged greetings and then I blurted out, "Do you think I should wake Mother and Daddy? Where are they?"

"They are at Anabeth's, and yes, you'd better call!"

So I called Tampa and talked to Mother on one extension and Annie on the other. Daddy was asleep, so I decided not to wake him. I would call back in a few hours.

I asked Anabeth, "Do you think I should call Vivian and Emi and wake them up?"

"I think you'd better, or your name will really be mud," was Mother's reply.

Those phones were truly lifelines for me over the next few days. As I talked to friends and family, the reality of what was happening settled in. In one conversation a dear friend and classmate from the foreign service said rather strangely, "Now, Kate, I am not going to ask you any questions, but I am willing to listen to anything you want to tell me."

That, I didn't understand. "Susan, what on earth is going on?" I asked.

She explained gently that some psychologist had said we might not be able to talk about what had happened and that we shouldn't be pushed.

All I could do was laugh. "Susan, you know me better than that. If you've got some questions, ask them." With that we settled back into our natural relationship and talked about the things happening in our lives. Her daughter, Katie, had been born during my captivity, and I wanted to know all about my namesake! She, in turn, wanted to know how I *really* was. I told her I was fine, just fine.

We were still making phone calls and getting in touch with our loved ones when former President Carter and former secretaries of state Vance and Muskie arrived to greet us on January 21. I was impressed with Carter's candor and his willingness to meet with us and answer our questions about the reasons for the long captivity.

His visit included a very special personal touch. After our group meeting with the president, there were so many members of the hospital staff who wanted to greet him that I decided to slip away to the telephone room. I had my head buried deep in the phone booth, talking to Mother, when I felt a hand on my shoulder. I turned around, and it was President Carter.

"Who are you talking to, your mother?" he asked kindly. "What is her name? May I speak to her?"

"It's Elsie," I said and turned back to the phone. "Just a minute, Mother. The president wants to speak to you."

He took the phone from my hand and started the conversation. "Elsie, this is Jimmy Carter." He added something about me. Mother must have asked how I was, for the next thing I knew he was saying, "She looks just fine, and I'm giving her a big hug for you right now." And he was.

After he had finished talking to Mother, he moved about the room speaking to the families of the rest of us who were using the telephones.

Our meeting was brief, but it left me with a deep impression of a caring, compassionate man. His attitude was even more remarkable when I considered the tremendous strain he had been under as well as what must have been his personal disappointments in not being reelected and not having us return during his term of office.

The invitations and the telephone calls from newspapers and radio and television stations began to pour in. Would we talk, could we do this, would we do that? Please, please, wouldn't we do an interview?

I received a telegram from the *Des Moines Register* asking me to call and talk with them, so I picked up the phone and dialed the number they had given. When I said, "This is Kathryn Koob in Wiesbaden," I heard a sudden stammer at the other end. But whoever it was made a quick recovery and almost shouted, "It's Kathryn Koob!" They interviewd me for about thirty minutes, and I remembered to thank the people at home for all their support of me and my family.

Everyone seemed to be concerned about both our physical and mental health. The press made much of the stories about mistreatment which were beginning to emerge, and everyone wanted to know how we had withstood the pressure of being held prisoners for such a long time. I was glad I was able to tell people I was all right, that I had weathered the storm. And when they asked me how I had managed, I shared how the strength of the Lord had kept me during this time.

I was delighted and relieved to discover, in a day's time after a full battery of tests, that I really was in good health. My appearance, however, was another matter. I needed all kinds of things from the skin out. And we got our chance. Arrangements were made for travel advances, and in the dark of pre-dawn the next morning we boarded buses for the drive to the local PX.

Inside we were greeted by personnel who had come in early to help us. For the first time since our release we heard the strains of "Tie a Yellow Ribbon 'Round the Old Oak Tree."

Almost in a daze, I moved from department to department. Clothes first. New undies, a fluffy robe, a suit, a blouse, scarf, jeans, purse, billfold. And then the luxuries: a tiny camera and earrings. I bought a suitcase to carry the items, and as I suspected, there were no shoes in my size (size 11)! One more thing to ask the family to bring when they met me in the States.

Finally we were forced to finish our shopping and board the buses—in the glare of television lights. Someone had found out where we were. It was a quick trip back to the hospital where I began organizing for the trip home.

After my dental examination, the chief dentist and his wife made it possible for me to be spirited off the hospital

219

compound, escaping the prying eyes of the news media; and for the first time in over fourteen months I sat down in a home, a real home, to talk and laugh with "ordinary people." It seemed so natural for us to share the faith that had kept us through various traumas in our lives. What a lovely reentry to normal life.

As I settled in more and more, I decided to make a TV tape. Craig Roberts, a Tampa news reporter who had worked with my sister, was in Wiesbaden, and we arranged to meet at a side entrance where no one else would be. So early in the morning I dressed in my new Air Force parka and my new jeans and walked out of the fog to talk to Craig for a few minutes. He asked about the yellow ribbon in my hair and about the yellow ribbons in America, and I said, "Yellow will have special meaning for me for the rest of my life."

I was amazed how one camera and microphone turned into almost a half dozen cameras and microphones even at that early hour. I left quickly to return to the safety of the hospital.

The only other TV interview I did in Germany was with Ann. We took part in a CBS special on the crisis, hosted by one of my long-time favorites, Liz Trotta. I think I would have gone just to meet her, even if I had had nothing to say.

We were shown the way out of the hospital through the basement corridors, spirited off the compound in a darkened van, and taken to our appointment with the CBS people. We traveled some distance to a quiet, lovely hotel where we had a delightful hour-long chat with Liz. It, of course, was taped, and later excerpts were used for the TV special. After a light supper, we were driven back to the hospital. It was fun.

Being in that hospital was a bath of love. There wasn't a staff doctor, an orderly, a cafeteria server who didn't reach out to embrace us, to help us. It was impossible to keep track of the flowers, cards, letters, and gifts that poured in for us: T-shirts, records, books, bells, food, dolls, even lamps. What joy it was to walk into one of the other wards and leave a bouquet of those flowers with other patients, or to go to the obstetrics ward to talk to the new mothers and be invited into the nursery to see the newborn babies.

One of the nurses said jokingly, "Take your pick!"

"I'll take one," I replied, laughing, "but how will I explain this when I get off the plane in New York?" It broke up the entire staff.

The hospital offered a time of thanksgiving, too, in an ecumenical service in the chapel. There we met some of the chaplains who had supported our families during the 444 days, and there I had the first opportunity to worship with others in our group, including Colonel Schaefer, Rocky Sickmann, and Barry Rosen. Each of us read a passage from the Scriptures and talked about the impact and the special meaning these things had for us.

Finally, amid the tumult of the press and numerous wellwishers from the hospital, we waved good-bye to Wiesbaden and climbed on the bus for our trip to the airport and home. We had been briefed on our return schedule, and arrangements had been made for our families to meet us at West Point. We received last bits of medical advice and posed for a group photo. We were reveling in our freedom, and we loved being "home" on that foreign soil; but it was past time to be with our families again.

Our flight home included a stopover in Shannon, Ireland, where we were met by Ireland's prime minister, a member of Parliament, and all sorts of people and officials from the airport. There was not supposed to be a press conference, but impulsively the prime minister grabbed Ann's and my hands and escorted us to the crowd outside to say hello.

Inside the airport, a lovely buffet table with sandwiches and delicious Irish coffee had been set up, and we had a chance to do some last minute shopping. My ring finger seemed so empty since I hadn't gotten my jewelry back—I always unconsciously play with my rings when I'm talking with people—so I bought a cameo ring, a lovely blue shawl, and a white tam to keep my head warm in the States. These

221

were followed by a warm sweater and gifts for nephews and nieces. All of us were presented Waterford crystal bells, and before we returned to the airplane, Ann and I were also given flowers.

Back in the air we looked at all the things we had accumulated and wondered how we were ever going to get off the aircraft. "Let's split up the bouquets from Ireland," Ann suggested. We distributed a couple of flowers to each of the men so they would have flowers to give to their mothers, their sweethearts, their wives, or whomever was meeting them.

Colonel Schaefer took the controls of the plane just before we entered American airspace, and we listened in amazement to the stream of good wishes coming to us from air traffic controllers and other aircraft as we crossed the Atlantic. We responded with a big thank you to the Canadians for their help in bringing our colleagues home. That story and how we beat the Russians in hockey, I decided, were my favorite pieces of news.

The plane landed at Stewart Airport in upstate New York, and once again huge crowds had lined the access road. Helicopters hovered watchfully nearby. As the plane taxied to a stop, my nose was pressed to a window. Where were Mother and Daddy? I couldn't find them in the crowd. Then I saw Mother's coat . . . and there was Daddy! The Marines went off the plane first, with the rest of us right on their heels.

When I finally reached Mother and Daddy, I couldn't say anything. The strain of the awful ordeal was evident on their faces, and we simply hugged each other, letting the reality of reunion sink in.

"How are you?" I asked eventually. "Are you really OK?" The answer was another long hug. After such a long, trying time, it was enough just to be together.

We moved with the crowd toward the terminal, Mother carrying roses I had been given while still in Germany and Daddy toting my flight bag. Mother began to introduce me

222

to other hostage families. I saw Ann and met her mother. I started to introduce my parents to Mrs. Swift but stopped in mid-sentence when they burst into laughter.

"Honey," Mother said, "we all know each other!"

Inside the terminal there were more introductions to people my folks had come to know and a brief welcome ceremony. We boarded buses for the trip to West Point. I found a window seat, with Mother beside me and Daddy in the row behind us.

The trip seemed to take place in slow motion. The windows on the buses were dark, so it was impossible for us to be seen unless we pushed our noses flat against them. But the route was lined with cars and people waving their hands and flags, yelling, jumping up and down. Dogs wore yellow ribbons, as did every bush and tree and twig along the side of the road. And the flags . . . everywhere I looked there were flags. On houses, on cars, in people's hands, flying from specially erected flagpoles and then an alley of them marching down each side of the road with one of our names affixed to each pole. Daddy's eyes were quicker than mine. I missed my name.

Then there was silence. There were eight flags flying, but not with yellow ribbons. They flew proudly at half-mast above a banner of black, a silent testimonial to the bravery and sacrifice of the men who would never come home. My heart missed a beat, and I reached for Mother's hand. We looked at those flags, and for a second the world stopped.

What normally is a twenty-minute trip took over an hour, and I waved at the continuous sea of people and cars nearly the whole time. Finally, we pulled into the drive of the Hotel Thayer at West Point.

The Thayer is charming at any time, but filled with welcome-home flowers and family it was heaven! My odd-sized room was filled with more flowers and goodies and piles of messages, mostly from the press, who were anxiously waiting to speak to us. I pushed them all aside and went down the hall to Mother and Daddy's room, where we began

223

to catch up on fourteen months of family affairs. The conversation was still stop and start, but it was so good to be home!

While at the Thayer, we participated in a beautiful service of thanksgiving at the Protestant chapel. The service was exactly the kind I would have written, incorporating some of my favorite hymns and Scripture passages. What a thrill to participate in it with all of the others. Worship in a community of believers. What strength!

Another event I will never forget was dining with the West Point cadets. We were barely off the shuttle bus when I heard a commotion coming from the dining hall. Once inside, I saw what it was. The entire corps was on its feet, cheering, stamping, and waving handkerchiefs in the air to welcome us. I still get goose bumps when I think of it.

During our three days at the Thayer, I also arranged to meet a reporter and photographer from the *Des Moines Register* and received a wonderful surprise. In the private back room of a café, Jack Halvorsen presented me with a scrapbook of clippings covering the entire 444 days. What a gift! He also got a story!

None too soon, it was time to go to Washington, D.C. My sisters would meet us there. We were taken to Stewart Airport, more quickly this time, and then soon, but not soon enough for me, our plane taxied to a stop at Andrews Air Base and I was moving down the steps.

Where was my family? Dutifully I shook hands with people in yet another receiving line and moved toward the crowd of waiting families. *There!* Finally I saw our crew: Anabeth, Mary Jane and John, my dad's sister Ruth, Vivian, Norman, and their children, Teri, Stephie, Jerry, and Connie and her husband Joe. We were all talking at once when Mary Jane, her eyes twinkling, said, "In your first telephone interview you said you wanted a Jesup sausage! Here it is." Out of an aluminum foil wrap came a lovely smoked sausage! I ate it on the spot.

Now I was beginning to see others I wanted to greet. There were the women who had been released: Liz, Joan,

Terry, Lillian, and Kathy, and there were the Lijeks and Staffords.

Such hugs and screams of joy! "Yes, I'm all right! I'm fine!" That seemed to be all I could say, for the first question was always, "How are you?"

We were taking lots of pictures, and then the excitement hit Anabeth. She almost fainted. She grabbed John, and he held her up until the emergency squad could take her to a quiet place. The rest and a bit of orange juice revived her; and as we moved to the buses for the ride to the White House, she rejoined us.

The crowds along the road to Washington were the heaviest we had seen yet. School children lined the route, and there were welcome signs, flags, and as always, yellow ribbons everywhere.

As we moved into the center of the District, the crowds got thicker and thicker until there was nothing but people as far as the eye could see. People were standing on platforms, barrels, and boxes and hanging from trees and lamp posts. There was a USICA sign—"Welcome Home Barry, John, Kate, and Bill!" We were on our own stomping grounds. People screamed and jumped up and down as they recognized us. "It's her. I saw Katie!" I heard one young girl scream.

I waved and shouted thank yous until my family pulled me back from the open window of the bus. But soon I was back at it. Slowly we wound through the streets until we pulled into the drive at the White House.

At the Pennsylvania Avenue entrance, my family was directed one way and I to the Blue Oval Room. When the fifty-two of us and Richard Queen were assembled, President and Mrs. Reagan came in. Bruce Laingen began individual introductions, and Mrs. Reagan reached out to shake the first person's hand. But halfway through the courtesy she said, "I can't stand this!" Then she threw her arms around the young man, giving him a big hug. The President followed, shaking hands.

They proceeded around the room in that fashion until they came to me. The President stopped, looked at Mrs. Reagan with a twinkle in his eye, and said, "Now, it's my turn!" So I got a hug from both of them.

There were ceremonies on the lawn with our families, after which we returned to the Oval Room where the President presented a small silk flag in a lovely rosewood box to each of us. We then moved into the reception rooms for coffee and refreshments with the numerous dignitaries who had been invited. I'm told more people accepted the invitation (6,000 were mailed) for this affair than for any other White House ceremony ever. We were officially home.

**Knob returns home
amid cheers, tears**
Des Moines Register
February 5, 1981

18

JANUARY 30, 1981

Next to the presidential welcome, one of the very beautiful and meaningful events in our homecoming was a service at the National Cathedral. There, with some of my colleagues and our families, we offered thanks to God for our safe return.

It was an emotional service, full of the praise that overflowed from all our hearts. Additionally, we asked God to bless and keep those families who had given their sons, husbands, and fathers in the attempt to rescue us. I was grateful that a nation that spent hours and hours on its knees asking for our safe return took time to give thanks.

When the service ended, Anabeth, Mary Jane, and I were whisked off to the airport with a number of other ex-hostages. Next on the agenda: a ticker-tape parade in New York City.

New York has always been one of my favorite places. I lived there for a short time in 1968–69, and because my sister Micki lived there for so many years, I love to visit. My friends who live and work there were excited about our coming, and the welcome they had planned was as warm as the welcome from the whole city. Nobody knows how to throw a party like New York! From the moment we boarded

227

our special flight, I knew this would be a memorable experience.

After an arrival greeting by Mayor Koch, we were ushered into big black limousines for an impressive motorcade to the Waldorf-Astoria. All along the way were cheering crowds of people. As we entered the lobby at the grand hotel, I thought, *This is just like* Hello, Dolly!

You may remember the scene: Dolly comes into the restaurant, and everyone stands up and greets her with wild applause. Then she walks, like a queen, down some steps to her table. Well, instead of walking *down* steps, we walked *up* steps. But all the hotel staff were there as we moved through a crowd of cheering, clapping people who made us feel like the most important mortals on all the earth.

It was absolutely incredible, and I loved it!

Where do I continue? They wined us and dined us at Windows on the World and at Luchows, where our menu was a belated Christmas dinner, roast goose and all the trimmings. A "retroactive" Christmas tree had been set up for us, and there were carols and singers. The festivities were late by over a month, but nevertheless a marvelous Yuletide treat.

We saw two Broadway shows: *Chorus Line* and *Sugar Babies*. *Chorus Line* was a special treat for me because a friend was working with the show. How fun to go backstage after the performance and meet Alice and exchange bear hugs. And how can I ever forget Ann Miller from *Sugar Babies* asking for *my* autograph!

The time in New York was like something from a dream. I certainly didn't feel I deserved the honors being bestowed upon me, but neither could I turn away from the people who were reaching out to us. One way to show appreciation for the support of so many people was by riding in the ticker-tape parade. The packed sidewalks, the banners, and the cheers were important, not because we deserved such attention but because they spoke of the healing of a nation. Patriotism and love of country had not had such a visible and emotional display for over thirty years. I was glad to be able to say thank you by reaching out to people, waving, and when possible saying a word of appreciation.

A bonus of my New York stay was the friendship that grew between me and the security person assigned to me. Detective Henrietta Lange was with me the entire time, and so it was a particular joy to discover she was a fellow Christian and a member of the Lutheran church. When we parted, I asked her to take some of the many flowers that had been sent, and she shared them with her congregation the next day. Since that time, I've come back to New York and have worshiped with her and her family in their church.

I returned to Washington rather unsure how to handle everything. Too much was happening too fast. Everyone wanted a former hostage to come and lower a flag, cut a yellow ribbon, attend a reception, shake a hand, go to a party, talk to a television or newspaper reporter. . . . It was difficult to sort it all out. What I *really* wanted to do was go home and see the rest of my family and talk with my nieces. And that's just what I did!

Micki, who had just returned home from a trip to South America with her husband, joined my parents and me in Washington, and on February 4 we took an early flight to Iowa. After a stopover in Chicago, where we were greeted by more friends, we landed in Des Moines at 10:00 A.M. We were asked to stay on the plane until everyone had left, and then we were met by a receiving line that included the Governor of Iowa, Robert Ray, and Mrs. Ray, Mayor Pete Crivaro of Des Moines, and several mayors and their wives from the surrounding suburbs. The main lobby was filled with people shouting "Welcome home!"

After a brief ceremony at the airport, we were driven in the governor's limousine toward the center of town. High school bands were out, people were waving signs—just one huge Iowa welcome.

Although it was bitter cold that February day, the governor asked if I would mind riding the rest of the way through

229

town in an open car. I'd purposely bought a warm coat in Washington because I knew Iowa winters could be wicked, so I said, "No, if I can ride in an open car in New York, I sure can do it in Des Moines!" We moved into an open convertible. Perched on the back between the governor and the mayor, I rode through the main street of Des Moines to the State House.

I was completely taken aback with an invitation to address a joint session of the Iowa legislature, and further to learn I was to be awarded the Governor's Medal for Valor. I felt I had done nothing extraordinary. I had done only what I had been taught all my life, and that was to do the very best job of which I was capable. I finally decided to talk about the things I had learned from my parents and teachers. The theme of my remarks became "responsibility."

First, I introduced my parents to the House and Senate—a very special joy. Mother and Daddy were there to see the honor that was conferred on me because of their faithfulness. I, in turn, was able to reflect my gratitude to two people who had given me faith in Christ and the values I hold dear. And I urged our state legislature to govern in a responsible fashion. I urged them to teach responsibility and to become models for young people by accepting responsibilities.

The joint session was followed by a private luncheon at the governor's mansion, and then my family and I were flown in a small plane to Waterloo, Iowa. Now I was *really* coming into home territory. Whenever I planned my tickets from abroad, I asked for a ticket to Waterloo, Iowa, the nearest airport to our farm sixteen miles away. I have extended family in Waterloo, and when I got off the plane I was thrilled to be met by Dad's cousin, Milton Roth, and receive from him the key to the city. They *literally* rolled out the red carpet!

Some of my high school classmates were inside the terminal, as were a host of other friends, relatives, and total strangers who were eagerly waiting to welcome me home. A quick news conference gave me a chance to say thank you to

230

all of them for everything they had done for my family while I was gone. After signing autographs and talking to countless people, we climbed into a van and drove home.

No matter where my overseas post, coming home for me has always meant being with my family. No matter which airport I land at when I return from an assignment, I never feel at rest until I've had a chance to sit down with family members. In Jubilee, I feel at home when my nieces cuddle up on the couch beside me as we look at a favorite book, or when we walk around their farm looking at the new pony, the ducks, the goats, the new calves and kittens—all the important personages in their lives.

The ubiquitous press was waiting when we arrived at Mother and Daddy's, but I spoke for only a few minutes before disappearing inside. As fast as I could, I changed into jeans and a parka and (checking first to see that the press had gone) headed through the familiar garden, all covered with snow, to my sister's house to see the little ones. There they came, bounding out the door: Susie, Carrie, and Diann, who was now three years old.

"Aunt Katie! Aunt Katie!" Diann cried, her arms stretched out wide.

"Diann!" I yelled, and grabbed her up with a big hug.

Her father looked at Emi in amazement. "How does she recognize Kate? She was only eighteen months old when she last saw her! She *can't* remember her."

And then we all realized that for days, Diann, along with her older sisters Carrie and Susie, had been looking at television and seeing Aunt Katie with fair regularity!

That first day home, I was satisfied simply being with those little girls, sitting at my sister's kitchen table, drinking coffee, answering questions, having the girls sit on my lap and then scramble down to get something to bring back to show me. I walked back to my parents' house through the snow and the cold crisp air thanking God for this wonderful country life.

There were all kinds of good things afoot. One of the

231

neighbors held a pot luck for our community, which meant a quiet, joyous time with the people I had known all my life. And on Sunday morning, there was a special service of thanksgiving at Zion Lutheran Church in Jubilee, the church that had been so important during my early years.

The church was filled with community people, family friends, some of whom had come from a distance, our Bishop L. David Brown, President Robert Vogel of Wartburg College, and his wife, Sally.

Reverend William Planz, my confirmation pastor, also was there. He related how the only resources I had had for three and a half weeks, before I received the hymnal, and finally at Christmas, the Bible, was what I had retained from memory. And he told how his pastor had charged him at his ordination to make sure the children memorized Scriptures in confirmation instruction. As he spoke, I once more thanked God for pastors who insist that people do the hard work of memorization, for teachers who insist that children learn lessons, and for parents who work with those leaders to insist the same thing.

The regular worship continued, and then, during the sermon time, I was asked to speak from the pulpit. I talked about the thankfulness I had for what had been given to me in Jubilee by a group of people who did the very best job they could, in living the life they had to live and in giving their children the excellent goal of doing the same.

A Communion service followed. As I knelt at the altar rail with my parents and my sisters, I thanked God once more for the precious family He had given me, for His grace to all of us, and for His love to everyone in that church. I prayed that His light and His love would be known in Iran and that His will would be done there. It was the prayer I had offered ever since hearing Pastor Bremer pray it during his visit with us in Tehran at Easter.

After church, there was a pot luck dinner in the church basement, and from there we moved on to Jesup. The school had been opened for a community-wide reception. There was a parade through town. Then in the high school, my high school classmates had assembled and walked with me into the school auditorium. I was presented with the key to the city of Jesup, and several people there talked about the events of the past fourteen months.

One of my classmates did a remarkable job in reminding me of my origins, offering me a log chain for all of the keys to the cities I had accumulated during my homecoming. The afternoon was marvelous, topped off with a dinner for my classmates in the community room at our local bank.

The next event took place at my alma mater, Wartburg College in Waverly, Iowa. (I claim the Class of '58, which was the year I received my two-year parish worker's certificate, and the Class of '60, when I should have graduated; the Class of '62 claims me because that's when I received my bachelor's degree.)

At convocation I challenged the students to use their time at Wartburg. "Make it work for you," I said, "to grow, to explore, expand, search, question, and challenge." During the time of my incarceration, a vigil light had been kept burning on top of Old Main, the oldest building on campus. After my talk, we proceeded outdoors and I gratefully pulled the cord, extinguishing that light.

Sometime during my visit the idea of giving my services to the college on a short-term basis was born. As an official staff member, I could travel representing the college and talking about things in life that had been important to me. The time was scheduled: between the coming Easter and the end of May. It pleased me immensely to think of being able to give back to Wartburg a small measure of the gifts it had given me.

After two weeks in Iowa, it was high time to get my parents back to a warmer climate. Several telephone calls and an airplane flight later, Mother and Daddy and I were at the Tampa airport greeting one more niece and nephew. I was almost bowled over by the reception from almost eleven-year-old Emma Louise. She grabbed me for a big

233

welcome-home hug, and affectionately refused to let go of me as we rode up the escalator.

I had thought the interest of the press had abated, but to my surprise, a whole new entourage of newspaper and television reporters was waiting for us in the airport lobby. They still wanted tc know what my plans were and how I *really* felt. They repeated many of the same questions I had been answering (and continue to answer) ever since I came home. Finally, we were alone with our Florida family. Neighbors dropped by to share a cake and a glass of lemonade and to talk, and I began to work on my correspondence. I answered hundreds of letters during those first days and weeks and still have thousands more to go.

So this was the homecoming: joyous because I was with my family and friends and an occasion of celebration because all fifty-two of us had come back. We were safe, we were in relatively good health, and we were reunited with our families. The nation had survived a crisis and, in my opinon, had done a good job. But homecoming wasn't just fifty-two American hostages being released. It was, I feel very much, Americans rediscovering a new sense of national identity.

As I listened to people talk about "The 444 Days," I marveled at the way our nation was drawn together. We held our heads high, determined that the actions of a group of militant students in revolt and rebellion, violating all sorts of international laws would not, and could not, drag us down to their level. Somehow, in all of this, we in this country were learning how to be committed to each other again.

EPILOGUE

"Who's calling, please?" Mary Jane asked.

Her normally warm voice had a crisp, businesslike tone. She had had phone calls almost nonstop since before my arrival in Washington.

Then she relaxed and laughed. "Yes, Mrs. Todd, she's here. Just a minute."

She turned and handed me the phone. "Kate, it's Susan's mom." Elsie Todd was a high school English teacher in Chatham, Virginia, the mother of my friend and my namesake's grandmother. We had become very close friends.

"Hi! How are you?" I asked.

"We're just fine. Susan was so excited when you called her from Germany. We heard all about it!" And our conversation continued, covering all of the topics beloved friends can find to talk about.

Finally there was a pause and Elsie said, "Katie, you made a dreadful mistake!"

My heart sank. *What had I been reported to have said now?* I wondered. "What did I do?" I gasped.

"You said you wanted to talk to as many people as you could," responded Mrs. Todd. I could almost hear the twinkle in her eye. "And my students said they want to hear you. Can you come be our commencement speaker in June?"

"I'd love to!"

That conversation was the beginning of my trying to say thank you. I have spent thousands of hours traveling and talking, signing autographs, answering letters and telephone calls, and giving press conferences. Many of these activities were simply to respond in a small way to the outpouring of love sent my way by so many people. It also gave me a chance to talk about The Simons Memorial Scholarship Fund.* I suspect the rest of my life will in some way be a thank-you for the special care given me by God and His people.

Since my return from Iran, people have favored me with gifts, awards, proclamations, and innumerable kinds of special honors. Every time someone asks me to accept such a tribute, or whenever a mother says to me, "My daughter thinks you are a real heroine!" I am humbled anew. I simply did my job the best way I knew how, with the help of my Lord. *He* is the one who should be honored. The best way I can express honor to Him is to be His servant.

I'm not sure where this servanthood will lead me, but it certainly has opened unusual doors for witnessing. Can you imagine being asked, first thing, on the *Today* show: "How do you learn to love your enemies?" It happened to me! And it happens regularly as I go around the country speaking and talking with people.

My desire to serve led to the writing of this book. I knew it would be hard work, and it was. But so many people have said in one way or another, "Just let us know how you did it." And I hope I've told you. If you didn't find anything new or different in my story, it's because the good news of the love of God is old, old, old.

When God created humankind, He gave us free will. When we abused that freedom and were removed from the garden, God in His love gave us the promise:

---

*The fund will be used to help pay college expenses for the children of the eight men who died in the rescue attempt. Contributions may be sent to Simons Memorial Fund, P.O. Box 8, Dallas, Texas 75221.

I will put enmity between thee [the serpent, or Satan] and the woman, and between thy seed and her seed; it shall bruise thy head, and thou shalt bruise his heel" (Gen. 3:15).

One day His love and power would be manifested in the Messiah.

Through the ages God has demonstrated His love and faithfulness, often contrasted with our rejection and unfaithfulness. In the fullness of time He sent His Son—His *Son*—who loved us so much that He gave His life for us. What a wonder! Knowing His love, having faith in His strengthening power, and relying on His grace was what kept me going day by day through those weeks and months of uncertainty.

That doesn't mean there weren't days when I was unhappy, discouraged, and blue. Some days I was all three—and some days I just plain rebelled. But I *knew* God loved me, and I was safe in His care. Not safe in earthly terms, mind you; we never have a guarantee of that in Scripture. Our safety is eternal in Christ.

Perhaps I say thank you best when I share the gospel of Christ. How *is* it possible to love your enemy? I still don't know "how," but I do know it is a command that I as a Christian can obey. That love, as the love I have for Christ, is a gift of the Holy Spirit, for "the love of God is shed abroad in our hearts by the Holy Ghost" (Rom. 5:5).

That miracle of love is one of the great realities I experienced in Iran. I had many teachers: Christ in the Garden, Corrie ten Boom, the Maryknolls, St. Augustine, Martin Luther, Brother Carlo Caretto. The prayer of Pere de Foucauld became one of my favorites:

> My father
> I abandon myself to you
> Do with me what you will
> Whatever you do with me
> I thank you.
> I am prepared for anything.

237

I accept everything
Provided that your will is fulfilled in me
And in all creatures.
I ask for nothing more, my God.
I place my soul in your hands.
I give it to you, my God,
with all the love of my heart
because I love you.
And for me it is a necessity of love,
this gift of myself,
this placing of myself in your hands
without reserve
in boundless confidence
because you are
my Father.*

This prayer verbalized the essence of my trust. There was virtually nothing I could do but trust and wait! Experiencing the love of God each day as I did was reason enough to commit myself anew each day to His care. Knowing I had committed myself to Christ helped me to endure each change of location, each day without contact. God would and did take care of me.

Let us not be mislead—it is not easy to dedicate one's entire life to the will of the Lord. We have been taught to be "responsible," and it is difficult to let go. Yet once I turned the fact of my imprisonment over to the Lord's will, I was free to move within those confines.

Since my return I have talked with many people who are living in crises. Those who have trusted Christ can say, "When I let the Lord decide, things begin to happen!" Their cancers haven't necessarily disappeared, their loved ones have not come back to live with them, but they are free in the love of God to face these painful realities, not hostage to fright and despair. They know the *joy*, the real joy of the peace that passes all understanding.

---

*While in captivity I copied this into a blank page of my New Testament from Carlo Caretto's *In Search of the Beyond*.

238

I logged more air hours in the few short months after January, 1981, than I had in all my years of career traveling. And in June of that year, I took up my regular USICA foreign service assignment (stateside for the present time). I found I needed more quiet time than ever in the return to "normal life." There is so much more now to learn about and think about in my relationship with God and my fellowman.

It isn't easy to find time alone to listen, to think, and to ponder the Scriptures. Yet without this, I become willful—parched and arid as a result of separating myself from the Living Water. When I stumble all over myself trying to go about "my" business, I have to stop and remind myself that it is my Father's business that needs attention. It is then I find a quiet time on the city bus in the middle of Manhattan or in an airport lounge, where I can think and listen.

I have come to love the still small voice that follows the storm, and as I listen for it the storm recedes. Christ is in my life. My thank-you takes that direction.

I love being near my family, having the freedom to pick up the phone and talk to them. I love sharing holidays, letters, and other good experiences with them. I rejoice in good health and am ever thankful my family weathered this storm so well. But I knew they would. For it was in the bosom of that family that I first heard the story of Jesus sleeping during a storm. When awakened by His disciples, He immediately asked, "Why are you afraid? Do you still have no faith?" (Mark 4:40 NIV). Together we had come through other storms, though none was quite like this.

So my message is nothing new, nothing new at all. Just that age-old story of trust, faith, and reliance on the promises of God:

God is our refuge and strength,
    an ever present help in trouble (Ps. 46:1).

. . . The LORD your God goes with you; he will never leave you nor forsake you (Deut. 31:6).

239

Be faithful, even to the point of death, and I will give you the crown of life (Rev. 2:10).*

God loves us and cares for us. We are His creation, and we shall be His in eternity.
Thank You, Lord! Amen.

---

*From the Holy Bible: New International Version. Copyright © 1978 by the New York International Bible Society. Used by permission of Zondervan Bible Publishers.